Tropical Fish
as a Hobby

Books by the Author

Handbook of Tropical Aquarium Fishes

Tropical Fish as a Hobby
(First and Revised Editions)

Exotic Tropical Fishes

Tropical Fish in Your Home

Diseases of Tropical Fishes

Encyclopedia of Tropical Fishes

Salt-Water Aquarium Fishes

Goldfish in Your Home

Aquarium Plants

plus scores of pamphlets

With chapters on "How Fish Get Their Names" and "Aquarium Genetics" by the late Myron Gordon, PH.D.

And a chapter on "The Balanced Aquarium Myth" by James W. Atz, PH.D.

Tropical Fish as a Hobby

A Guide to Selection, Care and Breeding
Revised Edition

by Herbert R. Axelrod, PH.D.

McGraw-Hill Book Company
New York   Toronto   London   Sydney

For my Teacher, Myron Gordon

Preface

The ever-increasing popularity of tropical fish as a hobby has given people a desire to learn more about these fascinating creatures. As we watch them through the glass walls of their aquarium home, marveling at their color and grace of movement, we naturally wonder about their native habitat, their food, their breeding habits, their temperament, and so on. It is the purpose of this book to give beginners and more advanced tropical-fish hobbyists all the information they need to maintain a healthy aquarium and to make their hobby more enjoyable.

The owner of a home aquarium takes on his responsibility with the pride and passion one would have toward a family of children. Actually, tropical fish require little care, but the few basic rules of care and feeding are essential to their existence. Those rules are presented here in simple terms, and can be applied to the scores of tropical fish described and illustrated in the book.

For quick and convenient reference, a guide to more than one hundred fish appears in the Appendix. Arranged in tabular form, it gives the popular name, scientific name, source of origin, reproduction type (live bearer or egg layer), aquarium temperature, disposition, and facts on breeding.

It is hoped that the advanced aquarist will find much information for his use in the chapters on fish nomenclature and aquarium genetics by the late Dr. Myron Gordon and in the chapter on the relationship between plants and fish by James W. Atz.

The author's experience as a teacher in the Department of Science Education, New York University, leads him to believe that this book may serve still another purpose—as a reference text for teachers and students of biology.

But whatever its use, the author will feel that his work has been repaid if the book helps to advance the interest of the hobbyist and of the student in tropical fish. There is no more absorbing hobby and no more enlightening example of the laws of nature and natural history.

Herbert R. Axelrod, Ph.D.

Foreword to 1969 Edition

In the nineteen years since I wrote the first edition of this book, the aquarium hobby has achieved substantial growth. From an almost "exotic" hobby in the late forties, aquarium keeping is now the second largest hobby in America, with 22,000,000 households participating.

This rapid growth in the hobby has enabled me to travel widely over most of the jungles of the world, and in the past fifteen years I have brought back almost 300 species new to science.

Along with the greater assortment of aquarium fishes, hobbyists have available to them, through pet shops, hundreds of new aquarium accessories at much reduced prices. Stainless-steel, slate-bottomed aquaria are less expensive today than they were fifteen years ago! Heaters, pumps, filters, and colored gravel look nothing like those available at the time the first edition was written.

Perhaps the greatest invention of all was the Miracle undergravel filter. This filter enabled *anyone* to maintain a crystal-clear aquarium without the disadvantage of having an outside messy box hanging on their aquarium. It brought the hobby to the masses with its simple message: "You never need change water again!" Freeze-dried fishfoods also helped make the hobby more popular, for you no longer need live worms for your fishes; the freeze-dried tubifex worms are safer and much less expensive.

Since the writing of the first edition, my teacher, Dr. Myron Gordon, passed away. I loved Myron as a friend and counselor, for he shaped my life and led me into tropical fishes as a means of livelihood and happiness. This new edition would not have been possible without him; nor would the first.

Contents

4. Other Egg Layers 114

5. Scavengers 134

6. The "Annual" Fishes 151

Tropical Fish
as a Hobby

Chapter 1
Rules for a Healthy Aquarium

The first thing to consider in starting a collection of tropical fish is the type of aquarium you intend to maintain. Several factors enter into its selection: the cost, the types of fish you are interested in, the number and size of fish for the space available, and the reason for keeping fish (commercial, decorative, or as a hobby).

The question of how large an aquarium to get is easily answered: Get the largest size practical. The larger the tank, the safer it is for the fish, because there will be less variation of temperature in a larger body of water. Large fluctuations in temperature over a short time are dangerous to fish; in their native habitat, which you should try to imitate as closely as possible, there is relatively little temperature change. The easiest method to maintain the correct temperature is with a thermostatically controlled heater. (See Chap. 8, pp. 176–189.)

Another reason a large tank is best is that there is less chance of the fish suffocating. Most people believe that the term "balanced aquarium" refers to a balance between the plants and the fish in regard to the production of respiratory gases. They are incorrect. The essential exchange of gases occurs with the atmosphere through the surface of the water, even when aquatic vegetation is present. Therefore, the size of the tank, and consequently the amount of water surface, is of vital importance. (For a discussion of the part played by plants in the balanced aquarium, see Chap. 7, p. 156.)

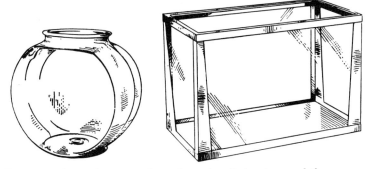

Two types of aquaria commonly used are the all-glass type and the metal-framed type. Having the same volume, the metal-framed aquarium has greater surface area, an important consideration. It is also very difficult to see clearly through the corners of the all-glass aquarium.

There are many types of aquaria on the market today with capacities from 1 pint to 50 gallons. Larger tanks, usually custom built, may be had upon special order. Most of the tanks larger than 2 gallons are made with metallic frames, while the smaller ones may be all glass. The all-glass tanks have an advantage over the frame tanks in that they do not leak and are easily cleaned, but they must be handled carefully to avoid cracking, and are harder to see through as the rounded edges make visibility very poor. When purchasing a frame tank, test it for leaks. Though there are special cements on sale that make repairing a simple, minor job, it is easier and more encouraging to start out on the right foot.

A good size aquarium to start with is a 10-gallon, metal-framed tank. This offers plenty of room for a dozen or more small tropical fish and gives the novice a chance to learn all the intricacies of fish care without going into the hobby too expensively. The tank should be equipped with a thermostatically controlled heater, a reflector, scavengers, and some sort of vegetation. These are the bare essentials for an aquarium. Remember that you are trying to imitate the native surroundings of the fish. The more successfully you do this, the more successful you will be with your fish.

A cover should always be provided for your aquarium. This should be a piece of glass—ordinary windowpane will do—cut to fit the tank. This will keep the fish from jumping out, will help control evaporation, and will protect the water from soot, dust, and other kinds of dirt. Moreover, it will serve to discourage prying creatures, be they cats or people! Do not worry about suffocating your fish; even the tightest fit of glass laid on the tank will still admit sufficient air. It is permissible to cut off one small corner of the glass for convenience in feeding.

The next consideration is light. As plants must have strong light in order to remain healthy and to grow, the aquarium should be placed near a window, if possible, so that it can get a minimum of two hours' direct sunlight daily. However, light from an ordinary electric-light bulb serves as well as sunlight, and reflectors for this purpose are made to fit all standard-type aquaria. Fluorescent lights are becoming popular and are equally effective.

Scavengers are a necessity with every tank, for they eat the food that is left uneaten by the other fish and thus prevent it from decaying and contaminating the water. Since the starting aquarist may overfeed his stock, a few scavengers will give him some leeway on overfeeding. Scavengers also help keep down unwanted algae that may grow on the sides of the tank. Some of the best types of scavengers are snails and catfish, although there are many other types, which will be discussed later.

The three hazards which most tropical fish face are overcrowding, overfeeding, and temperature change. Overcrowding exists when there are more fish in the tank than it can support. It has been found that there is hardly ever a shortage of oxygen dissolved in aquarium water but that there may develop an excess of suffocating carbon dioxide. When fish are too crowded, the concentration of this gas reaches lethal proportions. The safest

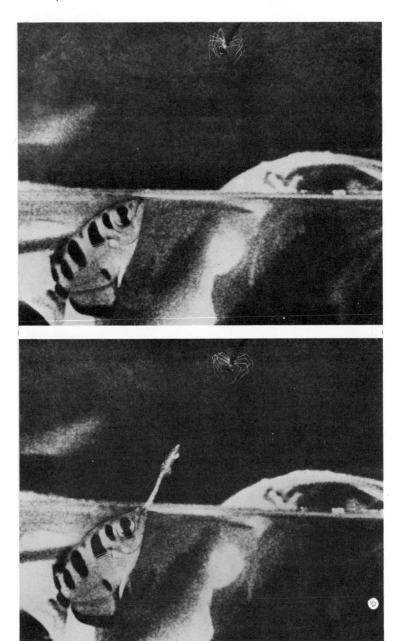

This remarkable series of pictures shows the Archer Fish (*Toxotes jaculatrix*) (1) preparing to make a meal of an unsuspecting spider; (2) spitting a well-directed stream of water at the spider; (3) hitting the spider; (4) leaping out of the water and snapping up the stunned spider. These pictures, enlargements of a slow-motion film, were taken in the sunlight atop the old Aquarium at the Battery in New York in the early 1930s by Pathé.

Argentine Pearl Fish (*Cynolebias bellottii*), a peaceful and beautiful fish from Argentina, has rarely been bred in an aquarium. Female on the right.

formula for spacing your fish, therefore, is to allow 1 gallon of water for every inch of fish. If you have ten small fish that average one-half inch in length, then you can safely keep them in a 5-gallon tank.

The water gives off carbon dioxide to the atmosphere at its surface; thus the surface area of the tank is another important factor in determining the number of fish that you may safely maintain in your aquarium. The larger the surface area, the more chance for the carbon dioxide to escape into the atmosphere. One of the dangers of a spherical or globe type of tank is that it has a small neck and not much carbon dioxide can be discharged by the water. To be safe, figure on a minimum of 10 square inches of surface area for every inch of fish.

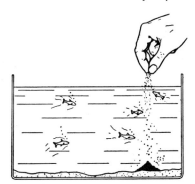

Overfeeding, one of the
principal causes of death
of many tropicals.

These precautions should be taken into consideration *before* you buy your tank.

A good understanding of the needs of your fish is important. When an aquarium is well prepared, it requires little attention— if you care to go on a vacation for a week or so there is no danger of leaving the fish behind without food; they can get along on the microscopic bodies that are to be found in every aquarium. You should by no means dump a whole week's supply of food into the tank and imagine that the fish will eat only as much as they need and leave the rest for the next day. Fish do not know how to ration their food; their code of survival is "catch as catch can," and they eat all that they find. Even if they did leave some over, the food would get stale and contaminate the water. Many more fish die from overfeeding than from underfeeding, so be very careful.

The best rule to remember is: *Feed your adult fish once a day and only as much as they can consume in ten minutes.* As well as the quantity, the regularity of feeding is important for the health of your fish. (Variations of this rule will be found in the discussions of the individual fish.)

There is quite a selection of food that is offered by many concerns. The author has found that a rotation of three or four standard foods, using a different kind every four days, is suc-

China Fish (*Channa asiatica*), sometimes referred to as "Snakehead."

Fresh-water Butterfly Fish (*Pantodon buchholzi*). A beautiful fish whose fin development reminds one of a marine flying fish. The Butterfly Fish, unfortunately, has an appetite for smaller fish and is not recommended for the community tank.

Worm-jawed Mormyrid (*Gnathonemus petersii*), from tropical fresh waters of Africa, is an aquarium oddity.

cessful. The live food that is prevalent in the fish's natural environment is also necessary as a part of their ration for a high standard of health.

Another important environmental variable is the temperature of the water in your aquarium. Fish are cold-blooded, and with very few exceptions (tuna and a few other very active fish), their body temperature is nearly the same as that of the water they live in. Tropical fish are accustomed to live in water that rarely goes below 65° F. and so they usually get along at the ordinary house temperature of 68° F. However, as the different species are accustomed to different temperatures, each fish must be considered individually. Sixty-five degrees is only a minimum. If the fish are expected to reproduce, some mechanical means must be used to raise the temperature of the water to the optimum temperature for breeding. To keep the temperature of the water as constant as possible at night, when the room temperature drops, and also to give the plants light energy for photosynthesis, insert a long-type 25-watt bulb about three-fourths of its length into the water, exercising caution to prevent short-circuiting and making sure that the water does not get into the socket. This process is not advisable, however, for tanks that contain less than 3 gallons of water.

Preparations for a New Aquarium

One of the first steps in preparing a new aquarium before introducing your fish into it is to clean it out thoroughly. Many tropical fish hobbyists use a rock-salt solution to wash out the inside of the tank. This preparation is simple and inexpensive. First, fill the tank with fresh water at about the temperature of the water that you expect to keep in it. Do not use hot water, as it may crack the glass or loosen the cement. Then check to see whether the tank is leaking—even if it was tested in the shop, there is every likelihood that it was jarred in the transportation to your home. Do not try to move the tank when it is full of water—a cubic foot of water weighs over 60 pounds. If you find there are no leaks, scoop out the water, leaving about 1 inch on the bottom. Take some rock salt and dissolve it in the water. Then run a small piece of cloth over all the surfaces of the tank. After every surface has been in contact with the salt solution, again fill the tank with water and let it stand for a few hours, leaving the salt solution in also. Then scoop out all the water and run fresh water into the tank for ten or fifteen minutes. Scoop this fresh water out and dry the tank, making sure that no large crystals of rock salt have remained undissolved on the sides. Although a trace of salt in the water is more beneficial than detrimental to the tank, too much salt has a toxic effect on the fish and plants. Salt acts to kill fungi and certain other disease-producing organisms and so aids in the protection of the fish. Do not use any other type of disinfectant in the tank; most of the others are poisonous

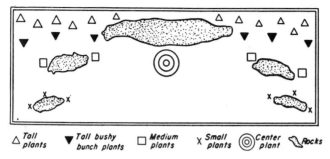

| △ Tall plants | ▼ Tall bushy bunch plants | □ Medium plants | X Small plants | ◎ Center plant | ⟁ Rocks |

Planting arrangements should be in a horseshoe pattern—tall plants and rocks to the rear, shorter plants to the front.

to the fish. Play safe and use salt. If rock salt is not available, any type of table salt will do.

The next step in preparing your aquarium is to get material in which to plant the vegetation. Pebbles, shells, marbles, and large rocks are not advisable, except for spawning purposes. They may have some soluble salts in them that would be dangerous for the fish and they will create spots which the fish and snails cannot reach, and thus provide a lodging place in which food may decay. A good rule to follow is not to have any place in the aquarium that the snails and fish are unable to reach should a piece of food fall in that spot. The plainer the tank, the better it is for the fish. Fancy designs in rock and clay have little value, though such rocks as granite, sandstone, quartz, or slate are not harmful and tend to give the tank a natural setting. Coarse white sand is the best material to use for your base. Do not use fine sand as it packs too tightly and the roots of the plants may not be able to penetrate it. Although, in general, enough sand to cover the floor of the aquarium about 1 inch deep will be sufficient, some rooted plants need a bed of sand from 2 to 3 inches deep to provide proper anchorage and root space. The best arrangement for sand distribution is to start your sand deeper in the rear of the tank and let it run shallower toward the front of the tank. This serves two purposes: first, all the debris and uneaten food will tend to roll to the front of the tank where it can be easily seen and siphoned out; and second, the sand in the rear, where most of the vegetation will be planted, needs more depth than the front of the tank, which should be left rather free of any growth. Actually, the best plan for plant distribution is the horseshoe type, where the planted vegetation is around the three borders of the tank, leaving the front and center free for a swimming and display area. The tank should never be cluttered with plants. Fish should have at least one-third of the tank to swim around in freely.

All sand must be thoroughly cleansed before being used. The best and easiest method of doing this is to put it in a large pot, letting fresh hot water run over it constantly for ten or fifteen minutes. Make sure that the water is running in under some pressure so it will wash all surfaces and depths of the sand. After the sand has been thoroughly washed, pour off some of the water, leaving just enough to cover the sand. Put the pot on the stove and boil the sand and water for twenty minutes. Then pour off the boiling water and wash the sand again. After it is thus sterilized, it may be placed in the bottom of the tank.

Water

Your next consideration will be the water that goes into your new aquarium. Water looks the same regardless of what temperature it is, what colorless salts or gases may be dissolved in it, or where it comes from, but chemically it may be very different, and the difference is very important to the fish that must live in it.

As an extreme concentration of chlorine is fatal to all fish, the chlorine used in many districts to disinfect the water supply may be a danger. However, the health authorities will not pump water that is too highly chlorinated, and therefore water that is obtained from the faucet will usually be satisfactory in this respect, though even tap water is toxic to some delicate fish. But to be

The Piranha (*Serrasalmus nattereri*) is one of the most maligned of all fishes. True, if molested they defend themselves with their razor-sharp teeth, but unless their prey is actually bleeding or they are very hungry, they are not very dangerous.

When they want to use them, Piranhas have a very serviceable set of teeth.

safe, allow the water to stand for a day in the fresh air and in contact with the direct rays of the sun. Before putting it in the tank, scoop out a glassful at a time and pour it back into the container so that the chlorine or other gases dissolved in the water will have another opportunity to escape.

Many aquarists prefer to use pond water, but it has been found that there are many organisms in pond water that are detrimental to the health of certain fish. The safest water for the beginner to use is tap water that has been aerated by the method previously mentioned.

The proper way to introduce this water into the aquarium so as not to disturb the sand is to place a piece of paper over the sand and pour the water slowly until the tank is about one-third full. Then take the paper out and anchor the plants in the sand. Planting is much easier with this method than when the tank is full of water.

Before entering plants of almost all kinds into your tank, however, sterilize them thoroughly in a concentrated solution of salt and potassium permanganate (purple crystals). This will destroy any harmful organisms which might otherwise gain entrance to a healthy tank. Do not keep plants in this solution for more than a few hours or they may be destroyed. When the vegetation is properly anchored, fill the tank up to about one inch from the top, then check again to see if the plants are still firmly in place. Some of the plants are very buoyant and are apt to pull loose from the sand. (Methods of planting different types of plants are described more fully in Chap. 6.)

Remember an earlier precaution: *Before putting any water in the tank, make sure that it is placed where it is to be permanently.* Water weighs about $8\frac{1}{3}$ pounds per gallon and, besides being quite a load to carry, the sides of the aquarium might be loosened and the frame warped if you move the tank from place to place. Many a time has the bottom fallen out of a large tank when someone tried to lift it off a table. Do not let this happen to you!

Now that the tank is set up and you have all your equipment

Lyretail (*Aphyosemion australe*), a peaceful fish from Africa which has been spawned in the aquarium, is becoming increasingly popular in England and America.

Fundulus chrysotus is a native American fish found in the southeastern states. It is a snail-killer and has been spawned here quite easily. The young are easy to raise and grow rapidly.

in place, you are ready for the thermostatically controlled heater. Check the correct temperature for your specific type of fish in the chart in the Appendix of this text. Caution: Be sure to test the heater first in a plain glass container (such as a milk bottle) by means of a thermometer to ascertain that the thermostat is set at the desired temperature. If you put it into the tank with fish before checking you may later find that the fish have either boiled or frozen to death.

Now, be sure that the temperature of the water in the aquarium and that in the container the fish are in is the same. If they are different, then they must gradually be made the same. If, for example, the tank has a temperature of 75° F. and the fish are in water that is 65° F., then you must lower the temperature of the tank to about 70° F. and raise that of the water the fish are in to the same temperature. This method can be used, however, only if there are no fish in the tank. Raising or lowering the temperature of water that contains fish must be done very gradually, by no more than 5° F. per hour. The best method of acclimating the fish to the optimum temperature is to place them in a glass container in the same water that they were in previously and allow the glass container to float in the aquarium. This will gradually change the temperature of the water in the glass container to that of the water in the tank. When you are sure that the water, sand, plants, and other paraphernalia are all up to optimum standards, and after checking the temperature of the water with a thermometer, then and only then the fish may be placed in the tank. This is done by merely tipping the glass container very slowly into the water of the aquarium, keeping the water from rushing in too rapidly, and then merely letting the fish swim out.

Handling Tropical Fish

A word or two about nets and handling fish is always helpful to the beginning aquarist. The fact that aquarium-accessories stores sell many sizes of nets, with varying sizes of mesh, should be indicative that different nets are used for different sized fish. In general, use a net at least 1 inch longer than the fish itself. Never use a dry net on a fish; let it soak for a few seconds. Sometimes a dirty net will become stiff when dry, which, if used in this condition, can cause serious damage to the scales of the fish and thus leave the fish open to fungus infection.

Fish can always jump out of small nets and fall onto the floor. This is usually not a fatal accident and, with proper handling by the aquarist, the fish may be replaced in the tank. There are several methods for picking up a fish from the floor. The easiest is to throw a wet net over the fish and hope that it will stick to the net when the net is inverted. Another way is to place a stiff, thin card under the fish and get him into the wet net that way. Don't be foolish enough to grab the fish and squeeze. If you use your hands, it is better to get him by the tail fin between your nails— at least he can grow another fin!

It should be mentioned that fish can sometimes fall from relatively great heights and not be killed. Sometimes they are just stunned and when replaced in the aquarium they "come back to life." This is probably the explanation for a lot of stories about fish which were found "dead" on the living-room floor and came back to "life" after being placed in the aquarium.

Sick fish should be handled with a special net, and the net should be sterilized in boiling water for twenty minutes before being used again. Diseases may be spread from one tank to another if these precautions are not taken.

General Types of Fish

The task of classifying tropical fish into categories has fallen into the hands of those zoologists who deal with fish, the ichthyologists. They are responsible for the technical tongue twisters given as names to the fish. The reasons behind the scientific sys-

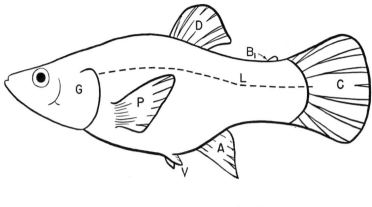

D—Dorsal Fin	C—Caudal Fin
A—Anal Fin	V—Ventral Fins
P—Pectoral Fin	G—Gill Cover
L—Lateral Line	B_1—Adipose Fin

Diagrams of typical fins of fishes.

tem of naming animals and plants are logical but somewhat complicated. They are explained in detail in Chapter 11, "How Fish Get Their Names," by the late Dr. Myron Gordon.

It is not too advisable for the beginning aquarist to sit down and learn all the names of these different categories for each family of fish, as they are mostly either Latin or Greek and may not mean much at first. But with later enthusiasm, and after hearing the names mentioned over and over at the different stores that deal with tropical fish, they will gradually become familiar and can easily be memorized. The Latin or Greek words are descriptive and give a clue to the type of fish. Some fish are named after the discoverer of their species. For example, take the common Mexican Swordtail. Its technical name is a combination of both the Greek word and the name of the discoverer. The name given it by the ichthyologists is *Xiphophorus hellerii*. *Xiphophorus* means "bearing a sword," and Carl Heller, the

Aplocheilus, sometimes called "Panchax," is from India.

Aplocheilus lineatus, called "Striped Panchax," has been spawned frequently.

discoverer of the species, had the honor of having the species named after him. The family name is Poeciliidae, meaning "many colors, variegated, and changing." From the original description of the fish we know that what the scientist who named it had in mind, when he called it a "sword-bearer," was not the long swordlike tail of the male fish, but rather its smaller, sticklike belly fin, known as a "gonopodium."

One advantage of knowing the scientific name of your fish is in ordering by catalogue; using the scientific name ensures greater accuracy in the filling of your order. There are about five hundred different types of tropical fish available, and the only way a large wholesaler or breeder can keep his fish straight is to use the scientific name; also a common name in one section of the country might mean nothing in another section. Most retailers and hobbyists use the common names; this may be the easier way out, but it may also cause confusion through improper use. If you learn the technical names of your favorite fish, the rest will come easily. (Check the Appendix for a complete list of the scientific names for your fish.)

To make differentiation easy, fish will be classified here in the following groups: (1) live bearers: those fish that deliver their young alive; (2) egg layers: those tropical fish that lay eggs and are usually the more colorful; (3) labyrinth fish: those tropical fish that have a labyrinth-like structure above the gills enabling them to take air from above the surface of the water as well as from the water itself (also called "bubble-nest builders" because the male of the species builds his nest on the top of the water, composed of bubbles in which he deposits the eggs of the female); and (4) scavengers: those aquatic animals that are kept mostly for the purpose of keeping the aquarium free of excess food and algae.

This grouping is by no means a completely arbitrary one. It is a grouping of convenience and will help the new hobbyist in his selection of the type of fish he may desire to keep. Each of these categories will be broken down further and fully discussed.

A handy reference guide to more than 100 fish appears in pages 264 to 283. Conveniently arranged in tabular form, it gives the popular name, scientific name, source of origin, reproduction type, aquarium temperature, disposition, and facts on breeding.

Chapter 2
Live Bearers

For the beginning aquarist, the live bearers are the most interesting fish to breed. With no particular trouble they may be propagated easily and rapidly. As is implicit in their title, these fish bear their young alive, the eggs having been fertilized within the female by the male. It was once believed that live-bearing fish are not truly viviparous (Latin for "live bearing"), but that they simply carry their eggs inside until they hatch. Careful studies have revealed that the female live bearer contributes to the growth of her offspring in a way quite similar to that of higher, warm-blooded mothers, and that her young receive nourishment and other vital assistance from her during their period of prenatal life. Unlike mammalian mothers, however, the female live bearer carries her developing young in the ovary, the same organ that produces the eggs from which they arise. There is no uterus in tropical fish. Another peculiar feature of practically all the live-bearing fish found in aquaria is that they can have several broods after a single contact with a male. For example, female Guppies have had as many as eight while being kept isolated from all males. This is made possible by the storage of the male element in the female's ovary.

One distinctive characteristic of most live bearers—and a number of other fish, too—is their habit of eating their own young, if the young are not separated from the parents as soon as they are

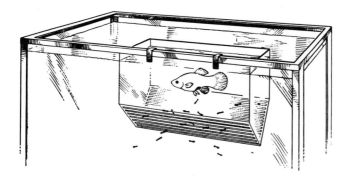

Live bearer dropping young in breeding trap. The slotted bottom allows the young to fall easily through the bottom and thus prevents their being gobbled up by an unsympathetic mother.

dropped from the mother fish. The breeding trap is a helpful device to keep the mother away from her brood as she drops them. This is a small container, constructed to fit inside the tank, into which the gravid female is placed. When the young are dropped from the mother fish, they fall right through the slotted bottom of the breeding trap and swim away into the rest of the tank. Some aquarists believe that these traps are rather dangerous to use, however, and that natural, dense foliage (such as Nitella) better serves the same purpose.

There is no difficulty in getting viviparous fish to mate. All that seems necessary is to have one of each sex in the same tank and they will multiply. The sexes are easily distinguished in this type of fish: the female has a fully developed anal fin, while the male has a round, pointed gonopodium, with which he fertilizes the female. Most of the viviparous young are matured and able to reproduce at eight months after birth.

If we attempted to set down over-all rules for breeding live bearers, we would be making generalizations that would be very limited and not at all helpful to the beginning aquarist. So we

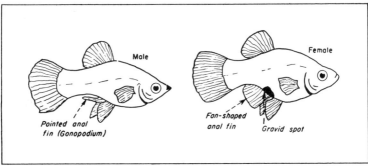

Pseudoxiphophorus bimaculatus, an interesting live bearer, is rarely seen in the home aquarium. This picture shows clearly the difference between the pointed anal fin (gonopodium) of the male (lower fish) and the rounded anal fin of the female (upper fish).

Sex determination in live-bearing fish is easy. Note pointed anal fin on male and fan-shaped anal fin on female. Dark gravid spot near anal region is often indicative of forthcoming brood.

shall discuss here only a few considerations that must be taken into account. It must be kept in mind, however, that they are only general and that a more thorough understanding for raising each species of fish is necessary. The specific breeding habits will be treated later in the book and should be added to the facts about the general habits of the viviparous fish mentioned here.

It is best to choose the fish that you want to raise according to their physical characteristics: size, color, and vigor. Choose only those fish with the best color. If you are going to take the trouble to raise fish, you might just as well raise good fish with color and stature that you will admire and which will be admired by your friends. There is a feeling of satisfaction and success that comes from raising your own fish, so add to this pleasure by raising fish that you will be more than proud to display.

When fish show signs of being "loaded" (a dark area in the anal region), they should be separated from the rest of the fish if possible. This separation has a dual purpose. First, it prevents the mother fish from being molested by the males that are around the tank; and second, it prevents the newborn young from being eaten by the other fish. The delivery tank need not be larger than 1 gallon, for as soon as the mother fish drops her young, she should be removed—or she will eat her young herself. The mother fish should be kept well fed while she is waiting to drop. It is a good idea to have the delivery tank heavily planted. Dense Anacharis and Vallisneria, with some Cabomba floating around the surface, will greatly aid the young fish in hiding from their parent, if necessary. Remember to take all precautions when shifting the mother fish from one tank to another. If possible, take the gallon of water from her original tank; if not, make sure that the water in the new tank is not more than 2° F. above or below the temperature of the original tank and that the pH in both is the same. The temperature should be checked with a thermometer, and the pH may be checked with a pH testing kit. (See Chap. 8, p. 8.)

After the baby fish are born, the mother should be removed

immediately and placed either back in the original aquarium or in a tank by herself. If she is put in the community tank, it is a good idea to have more than one female in with her, as a female is usually weak after she has given birth and is easily annoyed by male fish chasing her (especially in the case of the Guppy).

The baby fish should be left by themselves in their own tank for as long a period as possible, preferably until they are mature. If they are put into the community tank too early, they are liable either to be eaten by the other fish or else they will have a hard time competing with the older fish for food. After they are three or four weeks old, they should be transferred to a tank with rooted plants in it.

Baby fish should be fed fine, powdered food. This food is prepared commercially and is very reasonable. Infusoria (microscopic protozoa) should also be available to young fish. As the fish get older, they can eat coarser foods. Sifted Daphnia or freshly hatched brine shrimp are also excellent food for newborn fish.

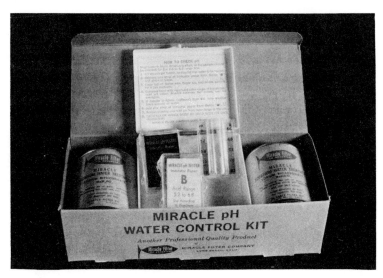

Test kits are available in every pet shop.

If you are having difficulty breeding live bearers, there are several possible causes of trouble that should be checked. If you have bred too often from the same fish, she may stop producing for a while. Sometimes the fish are undernourished. In this case, the best remedy is to feed them some live food and several varieties of dried food. Fine particles of chopped fresh meat are good. You should feed it to them a little at a time, because if you pour a large quantity into the tank all at once, some may get hidden in the crevices and start to decay. Another cause of breeding interference could be stale water or water with an improper pH. Checks should be made on the pH as well as the temperature, though the role the pH plays is not too certain. If all these causes are eliminated and the fish still fail to breed, then, in all probability, they are either too young to breed and may still have a few weeks to mature, or are too old. Old fish may frequently be recognized by the hump on their back. Compare them to young fish and you will recognize this physical characteristic easily. As mentioned earlier, the average live bearer matures at about eight months.

Guppy
(*Lebistes reticulatus*)

These are the fish to whom the entire population of tropicals owes its popularity. They have a long-recorded history, and there is evidence that they have been bred in this country for at least forty years. Today they are the least expensive and most plentiful of all tropical fish.

It is easy to see just how prolific the Guppy is by the following figures. If one pair of Guppies raises a brood, and they all live, and then this generation raises a brood, and they all live, and this process goes on for two years, there will be close to three million Guppies. Of course the Guppy mortality rate is high. Parents sometimes eat their young before they realize that they are drop-

FACING PAGE: Two male Guppies, *Lebistes reticulatus*. The longer the finnage and the more colorful the body, the more expensive the fish. (*Photo by Dr. Herbert R. Axelrod.*)

Note the beautiful fin development of this male Guppy. (*Photo by Dr. Herbert R. Axelrod.*)

ABOVE: This Veiltailed Guppy is from Paul Hahnel's famous strain, which has won awards all over the world. (*Photo by Dr. Herbert R. Axelrod.*)

ping them. Larger fish consider Guppies as tasty morsels. Besides all these natural enemies, improper environment, such as temperature and food, and other types of improper care, are also responsible for a large percentage of young Guppy mortality. But these fish produce such a large brood—every twenty-eight days when at their peak—that if only two or three thrive out of every brood, the proportion is not too bad.

Many experts in the field, even Dr. Myron Gordon himself,

started with a pair or two of Guppies and recommended them as the first fish for beginners. They are best for the uninitiated for the following reasons: first, there is more material and advice available on these fish; second, they are the most inexpensive fish that are obtainable; third, the males of the species are among the most colorful (many people call them "Rainbow Fish"); and fourth, they are hardy, and with proper environmental conditions they will live actively and breed often. Do not think that because they are inexpensive they should not be taken seriously. The information and techniques that you will acquire by taking care of Guppies properly will be invaluable when you decide on more expensive fish.

The males of the Guppy species are the individuals of the lot. There seems to be no two males colored alike, and there are few, if any, colors that do not appear in one or another of them. So beautiful are these fish that many have proclaimed them the most desirable fish to have in one's aquarium. They are timid, peaceful fish, but when a male Guppy dances in front of a female, displaying his magnificently colored fins, he is a sight to behold. The female Guppy is more stereotyped and less colorful than the male, usually a dull, silvery gray-green that blends perfectly with her natural habitat. She is heavier and longer than the male, running to about one and a half inches in length, while the males, though a few larger varieties are now produced, are seldom longer than an inch. There are many variations of the Guppy, the main differences lying in the shape of the tail—some tails have two or three nodes, while others are square or fan shaped. But a Guppy is a Guppy, in spite of the strains that have been developed. Some people believe that those Guppies with the swordlike tail came from a cross with the *Xiphophorus hellerii,* the fish commonly called the "Swordtail," but since such a cross has never been shown to be possible, it is more logical to surmise that this was just a chance development of the tail. Guppies have, however, been crossed with Mollies.

An interesting picture of a cross between a Molly and a Guppy. Several such crosses have been reported.

Guppies have an average litter of ten to fifty at a time—the largest brood on record, however, contained 126. These young fish, if properly cared for, will mature in eight months and be able to reproduce themselves.

An indication that a female Guppy is ready to drop her young is the black gravid spot on the abdomen. When this spot gets darker and darker, you may be sure that the time for birth is approaching. The spot is easily recognized, for the female Guppy is lightly colored in that region of her body. When the Guppy mother shows signs of being ready to drop, she should be very carefully removed to a tank in which there are no other fish and in which there is plenty of vegetation. The vegetation offers a sheltering place for the young if they should need to hide from the parent who, if allowed to remain in the tank with them, invariably tries to eat them. If the beginning aquarist has gone to the expense of a breeding trap, he may use that; it will save him many young. But the Guppy breeds so quickly that a few fish lost can be made up for in the next month's delivery. When the mother fish has dropped all her young, she should immediately be removed to another tank, preferably by herself so she will not be bothered by the male fish. Prominent scientists have made thorough studies of the sex life of the Guppy and have found that a male fish will try to fertilize a female fish even if she is placed in a jar separated from the rest of the fish in the tank, or even if she should be anesthetized and allowed to drop to the bottom. A freshly dead female in a similar position, however, would either be eaten or totally disregarded.

The young should be left in a tank of their own. They are pretty hardy at birth and can eat semicoarse food immediately, but it is more advisable to start them on regular fine food and gradually give them coarser food as they get older.

The proper temperature for the Guppy is about 75° F., though it may run as low as 65° F. and as high as 80° F. without doing any serious damage. Extreme temperatures are tolerable to the Guppy only as long as there are no large fluctuations over a short period of time; that is, do not let the temperature drop more than a few degrees per hour. The optimum temperature for breeding the Guppy is 75° F. This temperature may be maintained by the use of the thermostatic heater. (See Chap. 9.)

There is no narrow selection of food that Guppies will eat, but they are vegetarians to some degree and like fresh greens. The best thing to do for this green appetite is to give them some finely chopped lettuce. If there are plenty of green plants in the aquarium, there is nothing to worry about, as they will take their own as they need it. These green plants grow so quickly that they do not miss a little nibble here or there. Guppies also eat the standard dried fish foods. The ordinary prepared tropical fish foods are best and cheapest and will keep your fish healthy and active. Along with a variety of these prepared dry foods, the Guppies should be offered some live food, too; any type is suitable as long as it is not too large. A little fresh meat chopped into fine particles will act as a fair substitute for live food when the latter is not available. More information on the Guppy may be had in the Appendix.

Swordtail
(Xiphophorus hellerii)

The fish next to *Lebistes reticulatus* (Guppy) in popularity is undoubtedly the Swordtail, or *Xiphophorus hellerii*. Wild Swordtails reach lengths of about 6 inches, but aquar·um breeding has developed a smaller fish which is more suitable to the home tank. In the male Swordtail, the lower part of the caudal fin develops into a long swordlike tail, which serves as a positive identification for the sex and species of this fish. Since it is native to waters in and near Mexico, this fish is sometimes called the "Mexican Swordtail."

The Swordtail is subject to the same care and treatment of all live bearers, and as its temperament is much like that of the Guppy, it is an ideal fish for the community tank. The Swordtail has another feature that adds to its desirability, that is, its ability to be used in hybridization experiments. (Dr. Myron Gordon used them extensively in cancer research as well as in hybridization work.) The *X. hellerii* has been successfully crossed with the Platies, or "Moons" as they are commonly called. The Platies *(Xiphophorus)* are hardy fish and are also very desirable for the community tank. One of the many different hybrids that has been developed is the "Red Helleri," the final result of a cross between a reddish Moonfish and a Swordtail. The hybrid "Red Helleri" is a reddish-gold rather large fish.

It is remarkable how these fish react to their environment. One case is known where a female Swordtail was kept in a small tank with several *Betta* females—the *Bettas* are a rather ferocious bunch, although the female is less so than the male. The *Bettas* immediately chased the Swordtail around, and for a few days it looked as though they would kill her. Then, suddenly, they left her alone, and they got along very well. After a month of this rough environment, the female was put into a tank with a male Swordtail to mate. The female immediately started for the male and in

Wild-type Swordtail (*Xiphophorus hellerii*).

Female Swordtail which transformed into a male (left) and normal male Swordtail. Note the difference between the two fish. The body of the transformed male is rounded and full like a female, yet it has the "swordtail" and gonopodium.

The Simpson Hi-Fin Swordtail has been developed from a few specimens with exceptionally high dorsal fins which showed up in the hatchery of Mrs. Thelma Simpson of Gardena, California. (*Photo by Dr. Herbert R. Axelrod.*)

Judging by its "sword," this Hi-Fin Swordtail is still a youngster and promises to become a nice fish. (*Photo by Dr. Herbert R. Axelrod.*)

Swordtail with double gonopodium and caudal fin. Attempts to breed this fish were unsuccessful.

twenty minutes she had killed him. After a few days another male Swordtail was put into the tank, and the same thing took place. To this day the female has never accepted a mate.

Two lessons about fish can be derived from this case: first, they are quick to respond to their environment; and second, they have potentially many different behavior patterns. Together with a group of Swordtails, this female would probably have been all right, but by placing her in a rough-and-tumble environment, she lost all her timid traits and the more savage instincts apparently in her were brought out. Many fish of a timid family get very savage in a savage environment, and the reverse statement is also true. So keep an eye on all new fish that are introduced to the community aquarium.

The *X. hellerii* is an interesting fish to watch, especially when the male is "driving" the female. He will swim in front of her and then, with his swordlike tail erect, swim backward in a quivering courtship display. The male constantly swims back and forth about a female, always eager to mate. An interesting fact about the female is that at an old age she may lose her female characteristics and develop the secondary characteristics of the male, growing a swordlike tail and sometimes trying to court other females. This process of sex reversal occurs regularly in certain species of fish. In the Swordtail, however, it is apparently an abnormal occurrence, and the vast majority of such transformed females is infertile. By injecting hormones into normal female Swordtails, scientists have been able to change them to look and act like males, but these, too, are very rarely, if ever, fertile.

Platy, or Moonfish
(Xiphophorus maculatus)

The *Xiphophorus maculatus,* or "Platy," is the color king of the live bearers. These eye-appealing fish are more than just beautiful; they are peaceful, hardy, and prolific, and deserve a place in every community tank.

The first Platies to be imported from Mexico, the homeland of several beautiful tropical fish, went to Germany in 1907. Three years later, they are said to have been brought to the United States. In the short years that have elapsed since they arrived in the United States, more than a half dozen popular varieties have been developed through selective breeding—each more beautiful than the other. This process of selective breeding is long and laborious, but with the proper knowledge you can develop your own strain, provided you have the time and the space. Your reward in developing such a strain will be in the satisfaction that you have started something new. You may even have contributed something to science. Gregor Mendel will be remembered as the first one to realize, through his work with peas, that species carry certain characteristics from one generation to the other through

Black Platy (*Xiphophorus maculatus*). These fish are a healthy tank-bred German strain. Note the Nitella in the background.

Two male Sailfin Platies. They are both *variatus* Platies.

submicroscopic, discrete particles, later called "genes." The laws that Mendel formulated are applicable to tropical fish as well as to peas and humans. If you are interested, look up a few texts on the great monk Gregor Mendel and see if you would have the patience and fortitude to go through the same painstaking steps as he did to prove a scientific theory.

The Platy has been developed in many unusual colors and finnage; the gold-colored ones usually retain the name "Platy," while the other colored ones are often called "Moonfish" because of the crescent-shaped spot at the base of their tails. For example, your fish dealer may say "Gold Platy," while calling the colored Platies "Red Moonfish," "Blue Moonfish," or "Black Moonfish." Do not be confused with this terminology.

In the early 1960s Platies were developed from Simpson Hifin Swordtails as basic stock, which had huge dorsal fins. These Platies were called by various names such as "Sailfin Platy," "Topsail Platy," and "Hifin Platy." Nearly every color variety of *maculatus* and *variatus* Platy has been bred with the huge dorsal fin.

Breeding the Sailfin Platy is simple, though many of the offspring usually do not show the huge dorsal of their parents. A good strain might breed 50 per cent true; an amazing strain might breed 90 per cent true, but to date there is no strain that breeds 100 per cent true.

The prices of these beautiful Platies are considerably higher than the normal Platy, but they are well worth it, especially if you intend breeding them.

In 1965 I was able to bring back from Hawaii the first albino *variatus* Platies. In 1966 I found the first albino *maculatus* Platies in Hungary. These strains were bred at Gulf Fish Farms in Palmetto, Florida, where they were able to propagate thousands of these delicate Platies for distribution to pet shops all over the world.

Sex differentiation in the Platy is not a perplexing problem.

There is a marked difference between the physical characteristics of the male and female Platy which enables identification; the male is shorter and of lighter build than the female; also the anal fin is an indication of sex. In the female, the anal fin is fanlike and kept spread out, while in the male the anal fin is rodlike and is kept close to the body. This is the organ the male uses to fertilize the female and it is characteristic of almost all the live-bearing fish kept in aquaria. If you feel doubtful identifying the sexes, ask the fish dealer to give you two or three pairs and trust that his judgment is better than yours. However, do not worry as there is no danger of having either too many males or too many females.

Raising Platies is not too great a problem. The main obstacle is keeping the temperature constant, as the Platy is very sensitive to change. A thermostatically controlled heater is the best way to do this and it is indispensable with the Platies. A temperature of at least 72° F. is desirable, and 75° F. is the best for breeding, but whatever the temperature is, make sure that it stays the same. The best way to breed these fish is to give them an aquarium of their own. The Platy will rarely eat its young, and therefore one of the biggest headaches of the amateur aquarist takes care of itself. Most of the other fish will eat any young fish that swims and is small enough to be gobbled up, as well as their own young, so play safe and keep the Platies all alone in a large tank.

Females can have broods every four weeks, and, depending upon size, health, and breeding conditions, may drop from two to two hundred at one time, though they usually average about twenty. Care should be exercised with the female Platy, as she is as soft and delicate as she looks; when the time is near for her to drop, she must not be excited or moved. If you move her at all, you should do it well in advance of her expected dropping or you will lose her and the brood as well.

Food for the Platies is no problem as they will eat anything that they find. They will get along very well on the regular prepared dried food, with a little Daphnia or some worms now and then. Gordon's formula is excellent. (See Chap. 8.) They are partly vegetarian and enjoy eating algae.

All the different types of Platies can be crossbred, and the results of the crossbreedings are often remarkable. The colors will, in a sense, mix, and if the fish retain the correct gene combination, this color mixture will breed true. Of course this is sometimes a difficult thing to accomplish, but it is worth the effort.

Platies have frequently been crossed with Swordtails, and most of the Swordtails and Platies that are purchased are more or less remote descendants from such a cross. A purebred Swordtail or Platy is much more the exception than the rule. If you desire to try this cross, make sure that you have a large tank with plenty of foliage for the young to hide in, as the female Swordtail, as well as the male, will eat the young.

Platies and their close relatives the Swordtails, and the hybrids between them, have become regular aquatic guinea pigs for students of genetics. They are used in medical research because some of the excessively black hybrids, resulting from the cross of black-spotted Platies with ordinary Swordtails, develop pigmented cancers called "melanomas." This type of cancer is found in many kinds of fish and in birds and mammals, including man. No one knows what causes it in other animals, but in Platy and Swordtail hybrids it is known to be inherited. That is one of the reasons scientists are so interested in these fish. As a by-product of his investigations in this field, Dr. Myron Gordon has produced some beautifully colored normal strains of fish. His contribution to this book, Chapter 12, tells how this was done and discusses other features of the genetics of fish.

Young Platies are hard to distinguish from the young of other types of live-bearing fish. They are one of the most delicate types and are susceptible to all the evils of bad tank management. They will grow swiftly and be healthy if kept in the proper type of tank, with lots of room, a constant temperature, a normal pH, and plenty of vegetation. They will mature in about eight months.

Black Wag Swordtail, a variety first developed by Dr. Myron Gordon in the Genetics Laboratory of the New York Aquarium.

The following example will illustrate the importance of having optimum conditions for the growth of these young fish.

A typical brood of twenty-two was divided into two groups of eleven each. One group was put into a 15-gallon tank, which they had all to themselves—plenty of room, constant temperature, and live food every other day. The other group was left to their own devices in a tank of the same size but with many other fish. Of the eleven in their own tank, nine matured and reproduced in eight months; the group in the crowded tank took ten months to mature, and only two were alive at the end of that period.

Of course, separating all the young fish is a prohibitive task for the beginning enthusiast, but the idea should be kept in mind that it is better to have ten healthy fish than twenty unhealthy ones.

The varieties of *Xiphophorus* are mentioned in the Appendix. They need the same general care as the common variety.

Mollies
(*Mollienesia*)

We now come to the fish that are dear to the hearts of many people, mainly because they are found in many of the waters of the southeastern and central parts of the United States—for example, the waters around Miami are infested with them. It is not clear why this American fish was named after the Frenchman Mollien. These "Mudpussers," as they are affectionately called by the Floridians, are truly the fish for the amateur who is advanced enough to play with more interesting fish.

The reason for the complexity of the care of these fish is the fact that they must be maintained in water that is slightly alkaline or somewhat salty. It is impossible to maintain the pH of the water at a certain level, because regardless of how careful you are, there will be a certain amount of fluctuation. It is easier, and most frequently done, to maintain the pH if the fish are kept in a tank of their own, in which some sea salt has been added (1 teaspoon per gallon). The reason for keeping Mollies alone is that there are not many other types of fish that get along well with them and that can survive this radical pH. Since the Mollies do not usually eat their own young, if they are properly fed, the young can be left in the same tank as their parents; it is not too much trouble to keep them in a tank by themselves. Also, they do best in old water, so it is recommended never to change their water unless there is a good reason. As Mollies come in many varieties (differing in color, shape of dorsal fin, etc.) and are a beautiful species, a separate tankful of different Mollies is just as interesting as any community tank and is the best way to keep these fish healthy.

The male and female of this species are very nearly alike; the male has slightly more hue than the female, and since they are live bearers, the anal fin of the male is modified into an intromittent

Sailfin Mollies. Note the more intense coloring in the upper fish, the male.

Mollienesia latipinna. Note the appearance of the sailfin. The upper fish is the female.

organ. Mollies of the same type are very nearly identical, not varying from one another as do the Guppies.

The Mollies like to eat algae, and algae are an important part of their diet. If there is not enough light for a profusion of algae, they should be fed finely chopped greens, lettuce probably being the best.

There is no trick to breeding the *Mollienesia;* they breed frequently like the majority of live bearers. Since Mollies have the ability to control to some extent the time they will drop their young, there is no set schedule that they follow, and the female should not be disturbed or removed to another tank to have her young. The temperature of the water has something to do with it: 73° F. gives the best results. Broods of Mollies run up to 100, depending on the type of Molly. The young are free-swimming and will take small brine shrimp or Daphnia immediately.

A few singular types of *Mollienesia* are worth individual mention.

The Sailfin, *Mollienesia latipinna,* is really the true Florida Molly that earned the name "Mudpusser." It is the most common type of Molly and usually the most inexpensive. This fish has a large dorsal fin (uppermost fin on the top of the back) that is sometimes as large as the body of the fish itself. It is a greenish color with black dots, closely resembling a striped bass. Sailfins breed more profusely than any other type of Molly.

The Sailfin has been interbred with many other types of Molly. The large dorsal fin seems to be a dominant characteristic because, in interbreeding the Sailfin with other types of Mollies, it has been found to breed true, while other characteristics of the original have disappeared. Successful crossbreeding between the Guppy and the Molly has also been reported.

Another popular type of Molly is the Black Molly, or Midnight Molly. This fish gets its name from its velvety black color, and may belong to the previously mentioned species, the Sailfin, or to the following one, since black strains of both these species are known.

A fish of increasing popularity is *M. sphenops*. As their name, *sphenops,* implies, these fish have wedge-shaped faces and look quite pugnacious. The true *M. sphenops* is sometimes hard to distinguish from the other species of the genus *Mollienesia*. Color is no indication, as their color range is quite extensive, nor can they be recognized by their size and disposition, as these are also varied. (It is quite common for the commercial fish dealer to sell certain types of odd-sized or colored Mollies for true *M. sphenops*.) About the easiest way to differentiate between the *M. sphenops* and the *M. latipinna* is by the location of the dorsal fin. The dorsal fin in *M. sphenops* is set toward the rear of the hump in the back, while in *M. latipinna* the dorsal fin is set in front of the hump. The *M. sphenops* are usually very good jumpers, but it has been the author's experience that they are not so desirable as the more peaceful members of their family. They have a nervous, tense disposition.

Since its development by Yam Ming in Singapore in 1954, the Lyretail Molly has become an established strain in every country of the world. Lyretail Mollies are available in marble, green, black, chocolate, and albino varieties, and they certainly seem to be a dominant enough characteristic to be able to show themselves in early crossings with any established strain.

In Florida, where Mollies are raised in huge dirt pools, most major growers have found that they do well by dedicating a few dozen pools to the raising of various strains of Lyretail Mollies since the throwbacks are normal Mollies in the particular strain to which that pool is entrusted. That means that a pool of black Lyretail Mollies will have throwbacks which will be black normal Mollies, certainly a fish which can be sold and which will not harm the basic strain. Were the case that black Lyretail Mollies threw green babies as throwbacks, it would contaminate the basic strain.

It is interesting to note that the first Lyretail Mollies were green Mollies raised in the small concrete vats which most Far Eastern fish farmers use for intensive fish cultivation.

Black or Midnight Molly. Lower fish is male. Compare anal fins of male and female.

As Lyretail Mollies grow older, they begin to lose the lyretail in many strains with which I have experimented. It seems that the tail is most lyre-shaped when the fish is less than one year old. As the fish gets older, the tail gets fuller and the top and bottom extensions seem to atrophy and finally disappear.

There seems to be extensive sex reversal among Lyretail Mollies, more so than among normal blacks and greens.

Many hobbyists write to me and inquire about red Mollies. To date there is no such strain known. There are albino Mollies with red eyes, but there are no red Mollies in the same sense as

A Lyretailed Black Sailfin Molly. (*Photo by Dr. Herbert R. Axelrod.*)

A Mottled Lyretailed Sphenops Molly. This photo was made in Czechoslovakia by Rudolf Zukal.

A pair of Lyretailed *Mollienesia velifera*. The bushy anal fins make it difficult to differentiate between males and females. In this case the upper fish is the female and the bottom male. (*Photo by Mr. Low Check Long, ARPS.*)

red Swordtails or red Platies. There is no reason why a sport might not appear which will be red and might be crossed back into a normal strain to produce reds in future generations, but at the present writing it does not seem that any reds have appeared as mutants or sports among the many millions of Mollies which are raised in Florida, Singapore, and Hong Kong every year.

Feeding Mollies in captivity is a great art and requires constant attention. If you feed your Mollies a normal diet of the typical fish foods available at a variety store, you'll be doomed to stunted Mollies. Mollies must have certain foods in their diet if they are to grow at a maximum rate.

Most Mollies require algae, preferably Chlorella algae, which are soft and very digestible with an extremely high vegetable protein content, along with crustaceans such as Daphnia and brine shrimp, and fleshy meat such as Tubifex worms. Though this sounds like a difficult diet to obtain, there are a variety of foods available at your pet shop which supply these requirements. Miracle worms with Chlorella is one food which is a freeze-dried product made of Tubifex worms and algae. The freeze drying removes all the water and preserves most of the food value. Experiments I conducted using Miracle worms with Chlorella and Daphnia gave me better growth than when I fed the live equivalents. The freeze drying process kills all the parasites which are harmful to fishes and is to be preferred over live Tubifex.

Other Live Bearers: Gambusia

The Gambusia has been collected all along the southeastern coast of the United States. In appearance it resembles the Guppy, but in disposition they are as alike as day and night. The Gambusia is usually pugnacious and is not recommended for the community tank.

Gambusia affinis, the best known of all the Gambusias, has established quite a reputation for itself in medical and public-health circles. Because it has proved to be such an efficient destroyer of mosquito larvae, it has been introduced into no less than seventy different countries to help control these pests. Since mosquitoes carry such dreadful diseases as malaria and yellow fever, spreading them as they bite and suck blood, the Gambusia is undoubtedly the most important fish in preventive medicine. It is both hardy and prolific and will live in lakes, ponds, ditches, streams, mudholes, in fact almost any body of fresh water. There are numerous Gambusia spread throughout the United States, Mexico, the West Indies and Central America. Although it is a warm-water fish, special cold-resistant strains have been established as far north as Chicago.

Some Gambusia are black spotted, but there is generally so little difference between species that it would serve little value to discuss the distinguishing features of these fish here.

In breeding, they follow the general rules of live bearers. The optimum temperature for their breeding is about 75° F., but they fare well at 5 or 10 degrees above or below. These fish have a rather fond taste for their own young, so if it is at all possible, separate the female before she is ready to drop her young. Fortunately, the young grow very rapidly, and after the first week or so they are too large for the parent to eat, so the best practice has been to leave them alone with her in a large tank that is densely vegetated, and hope that they will last the week. Keep plenty of live food in the tank, also, when there are young fish there.

Feeding the Gambusia is no problem at all. They have an appetite for almost any live food and they also do very well on the standard prepared foods. Gordon's formula (see p. 188) is recommended.

As mentioned before, these fish are very hardy and prolific. They are not known to be particularly susceptible to any disease and, barring their ferocious nature, can be classified as a very desirable fish, especially for outdoor pools.

In large lakes they are extremely valuable. Their prolificness tends to keep the larger game fish well stocked with live food, while they themselves tend to eat all the undesirable beetles, larvae, and what-have-you that are usually found in most lakes.

The Cuban variety of Gambusia, *G. punctata,* is quite different from the types described above. They are more susceptible to discomfort from temperature change and not so prolific as their relatives.

Heterandria formosa

Another American fish worth mentioning, and recommended for the home aquarium, is the *Heterandria formosa.* It is outstanding in many ways. One of its distinctions is that it is undoubtedly the smallest of all live bearers. The mature male is only half an inch long—and is distinguished from the female by its telltale anal fin;

Poecilistes pleurospilus is a small live bearer sometimes used in the war against mosquitoes. It is easily raised in the home aquarium and is fairly peaceful.

the female may be an eighth to a quarter of an inch longer than the male. This fish has been given the name "Mosquito Fish," perhaps because of its size, but mainly because of its importance as one of the three types (along with the Guppy and the Gambusia) of fish that are used for mosquito-larvae destruction.

The life cycle of the mosquito is an interesting one. The larvae and pupae of the mosquito are aquatic and wriggle around in the water. After a certain length of time, they go through a complete metamorphosis and fly away as full-grown mosquitoes. Once the insects have left the water, there is no practical means of disposing of them in great numbers, but while they are in the aquatic stage, there are several techniques. One is to pour oil on the water so that, when they come to the surface to breathe atmospheric oxygen, the oil slick will suffocate them. This method has its drawbacks, as it presents a fire hazard, frequently destroys other wild-life besides mosquitoes, is unsightly, and also must be done several times a season. An alternative method is being developed now of spraying with chemicals, but this method also has its disadvantages. The third method (there undoubtedly are more, but they are all variations of these three) is to infest the water with fish that will eat the young mosquitoes. This need be done only once, as the fish, instead of becoming less effective as the chemical measures do, multiply and become more effective. The fish can eat their weight in mosquito larvae. Many aquarists actually bring mosquito pupae into their homes and feed them to the fish. But the problem of how to become rid of the mosquitoes once they have hatched is another story.

The breeding habits of the *H. formosa* are quite remarkable. The female drops a few fish every day; this feat may go on for a few weeks at a time. If there are quite a few females in the tank, you will probably find two or three new offspring every day. Sufficient vegetation should be provided in which the young can hide.

The optimum temperature for the breeding of these fish is about 70° F., and, as is true of the majority of fish, they fare better when kept only with members of their own family.

Dermogenys pusillus

The Halfbeak is an interesting little live-bearing species from the East Indies. It generally occurs in semi-brackish waters, and the addition of a teaspoonful of salt to each gallon of the water is distinctly beneficial. Males have a constant "chip-on-the-shoulder" attitude and are fond of staging battles, which seldom end in injury. The lower jaw is immovable, and the fish usually feeds by taking food from the water's surface and clamping down the upper jaw on it. Dry foods are not taken with any great relish, and small insects such as Wingless Fruit Flies are gobbled greedily.

A pair of Halfbeaks, *Dermogenys pusillus*, male above. (*Photo by Milan Chvojka.*)

Females give birth to about twenty-five young, with the pregnancy lasting twenty-eight to thirty days. They should be given a separate tank which is heavily planted when their time comes, because many of the youngsters are otherwise eaten.

The main difficulty in keeping Halfbeaks is providing them with a proper diet. In their home waters they get most of their nourishment by snapping at insects at or near the water's surface, and their tank must be kept covered at all times. They should be provided with small insects if possible, and Wingless Fruit Flies are a good item here. Some breeders get very good results providing their Halfbeaks with newly hatched Anabantids such as Paradise Fish, Blue Gouramis, etc.

This discussion has included all the live bearers that the average aquarist is liable to encounter; the Appendix gives information about those less frequently found. For fuller information about any particular type of fish, or for general information, see your fish dealer, or write to one of the larger concerns in one of the large cities.

Chapter 3
Egg Layers

The fish just discussed are viviparous like human beings, that is, they reproduce by bearing live young. Chickens typify another kind of reproduction, in which the female lays eggs which have been fertilized by the male by physical contact with the hen before they are laid; the hen then incubates the eggs until they hatch. There are relatively few fish which reproduce in this latter manner, that is, by laying fertile eggs that have come in contact with the milt, or male element, while still inside the female.

In the vast majority of fish, other than the live bearers, fertilization takes place outside in the water surrounding the parents. The female either freely drops her eggs or carefully deposits them on some object such as a stone or the leaves of underwater plants. The male follows her, dropping his milt on the eggs, fertilizing them. Those who are familiar with the blood spots in chicken eggs can realize the difference between fertilized and unfertilized eggs. An unfertilized egg can never hatch out.

Siamese Fighting Fish
(*Betta splendens*)

Let us examine closely the actual reproductive process of one of the most famous fish of the aquarium, the Siamese Fighting Fish (*Betta splendens*).

Siamese Fighting Fish (*Betta splendens*). The male *Betta* is truly a sight to behold.

The *Betta* is probably the most beautiful fish that ever adorned an aquarium, and one of the fiercest. It has been bred in many different colors and, owing to its popularity, will probably continue to be the subject of much experimental breeding. The male, as in most vertebrates, is the more gaily colored and pugnacious. He is distinguishable from the female of the species by his long-flowing, deeply colored fins that sometimes reach well over an inch in length. The female is seldom as colorful as the male and never has fins that can be compared in size or beauty with those of the male.

The reproductive habits of the *Betta* are *most* interesting. As is true of most egg layers, the *Bettas,* both male and female, must be conditioned for their orgy of reproduction. This conditioning process is a very old one, having long been used by hobbyists with many types of birds, fish, and animals. It is as follows: The male and female are put in the same tank, being separated only by a glass partition (many aquarists make their own tanks of this type, but *Betta* tanks arranged just for this purpose are on the market). The male tries vigorously to reach the female, and the courting begins. The more frustrated he gets the more beautiful and deep his colors become; he really defies description. His dance is one to behold; with his gills expanded and the look of a killer on his face, he dashes madly against the glass, trying vainly to get to the female.

Fortunately enough, after hours or sometimes days, he stops this mad capering and starts to build a bubble nest. This bubble nest is a work of art. First, the male *Betta* gulps air from the surface of the water, "chews" on it for a second, and then blows out a mucous bubble. This process is repeated hundreds of times until a nest of about an inch and a half in diameter is constructed. The nest may be high enough to be raised out of the water and sometimes reaches a thickness of about a half inch. After the nest is complete, it is time for the glass partition to be removed. But first you must be sure the female is ready for the male. This is not easy for the amateur to decide, as it must be ascertained that the female has eggs to be fertilized. It will be noted that if the female is ready, she will seem a lot heavier and fuller than before the seasoning process, owing to the many eggs that she is about to drop. When you are sure that it is time, the partition should be lifted out very carefully so as not to destroy the bubble nest, and the male and female should be allowed to have their romance. This is by no means the end of the story.

When the male sees the female, he will make a headlong dive for her, maybe ripping off a piece of her tail or fin in his clumsy attempts. The female will probably hide in the foliage that must be provided on one end of the breeding tank just for this purpose. The rest of the tank must be free from any other material, including sand.

The male *Betta* (the lighter of the two fish) wraps his body around the female. This is not a haphazard arrangement, since there must be an approximate coincidence of their genital pores so that the eggs coming from the female will be fertilized. (*Courtesy American Museum of Natural History.*)

The male has squeezed the eggs from the body of the female *Betta*, fertilizing each egg as it comes out. (*Courtesy American Museum of Natural History.*)

The male *Betta,* leaving the prostrate floating body of the female, catches the falling eggs in his mouth, preparatory to blowing them into his nest. (*Courtesy American Museum of Natural History.*)

The male *Betta* blows the eggs into his bubble nest. (*Courtesy American Museum of Natural History.*)

After a few hours of what looks like a rough fight, with the male chasing the female all around the tank, ripping her scales and fins to shreds, they will finally settle down. Fertilization requires that the genital pores of the male and female *Betta* be close together during spawning, as the male fertilizes the eggs as they are dropped. The male will wrap his body around the female and squeeze her until some eggs drop out, then he will quickly release her and go down for the eggs and catch them in his mouth. As the eggs that the female drops are very small and sand colored, it is obvious why there must be no sand on the bottom of the breeding tank. If the eggs should reach the bottom before the male has a chance to get them all up, they will be lost.

After the male has a mouthful of eggs, he blows them into his bubble nest and then returns to his bride for more squeezing, and consequently more eggs. This process may take hours or days, but should never take more than two days, since the fertilized eggs will start to hatch by that time. After the female has given up all her eggs, she must be removed, or the male will surely kill her. Then the male can be left alone with the hatching fry for a few days.

One of the functions of the bubble nest is undoubtedly to keep the fry up near the surface of the water, where it is well aerated. The *Betta* often lives in stagnant water, and it is entirely conceivable that the eggs, which are heavier than water, would otherwise sink toward the bottom where they would smother. Should a fry get too active and fall to the bottom, the father *Betta* is waiting to catch it and blow it back to the top. He may need to continue doing this for as long as ten to twelve days. To prevent his starting to eat the young fry after this period of time, he should be removed after ten days.

When the fry have hatched out, they must be fed Infusoria. Infusoria culture may be purchased in special pills, which, when placed in water, will dissolve and release millions of microscopic animals—rotifers, paramecia, amoebae, and many others—that

The Libby Betta male has fins longer than its body.

swim around the water. Strictly speaking, some of these animals are not Infusoria, but nevertheless they are contained in Infusoria pills. Fish of all ages thrive on them.

The Libby Betta

The most outstanding strain of *Betta splendens* today is the Libby Betta bred by Warren and Libby Young of Little Falls, New Jersey. The Youngs have concentrated their efforts on developing a strain of Siamese Fighting Fish which were the best to be found anywhere. They encountered some difficulties which were not insurmountable, and have arrived at four rules which they consider essential:

1. Use absolutely clean water, especially for young fish. Change the water twice a week whether it looks dirty or not.

2. Don't use unseasoned water. Store in a wooden barrel or some such container for at least three days before using it.

3. Use water that is as close to neutral (pH 7.0) as possible. The Youngs' tap water is 7.8 and must be corrected before using.

4. Use water as soft as possible. The Youngs use a commercial zeolite softener that brings the water hardness down to 2° or 3°.

By the relentless use of these rules Warren and Libby Young have been able to produce fish which are the envy of all who see them. Contrary to what many believe, they have no "secret" methods. All that they will tell you is to observe their four rules and, most important of all, *keep working at it!*

Paradise Fish
(*Macropodus opercularis*)

A fish second in popularity to the *Betta* is the Paradise Fish. Known to the technical world as *Macropodus opercularis,* this fish has had a lot to do with the increase in the fashion of home aquaria.

The Paradise Fish might be called the "Guppy of the egg layers." Its ability to survive dirty water, extremes of temperature, and poor feeding conditions, coupled with its easy temperament and beautiful color during mating time, makes it a very desirable fish for the community tank. It breeds exactly the same as the *Betta,* but in contrast to the *Betta* a domestic Paradise Fish is never so vicious and will seldom attack the female after she has spawned.

Many people keep Paradise Fish in their outdoor pools during the summer months. Temperatures as low as 50° F. and as high as 90° F. seem to have little effect upon their well-being, though temperature and environmental conditions do affect their breeding habits.

Strains of this fish have been noted to· breed true once a pure line has been developed. The Albino Paradise, with its contrasting pink eyes and reddish sides, is at present a very popular strain, and breeds true.

A caution should be sounded about mixing the Paradise Fish with Goldfish: if they are not in a large pool, keep them separated. The Paradise Fish seem to be jealous of the Goldfish's flowing fins and they see to it that they do not stay flowing very long.

Dwarf Gourami
(*Colisa lalia*)

The *Colisa lalia,* or Dwarf Gourami, is another fish that has gained many fans. Since it is the smallest of the Gouramis, it is very desirable in the smaller aquarium. But this is not the only reason for its popularity. The Dwarf Gourami is one of the prettiest members of its group. Like the *Betta,* it builds a bubble nest, but it goes one step further than the *Betta* in nest building and it weaves in bits of plants as a sort of superstructure. Owing to the added complexity of the work of nest building, it is rather common for the female to help the male in the construction, though frequently she meets death as her reward during the period following mating. As two strange fish thrown together for mating may not get along too well, it would be wise to observe the same precautions with the *C. lalia* as you would when mating the *Betta.*

The shyness and timidity of *C. lalia* may cause its keeper some concern, but these undesirable characteristics may be overcome by keeping them hungry for a while and then introducing some friendly fish into the tank. When you throw a little food into the front of the tank, the friendly fish will race for it, while the shy *C. lalia* will stay hungry. After a few days of this treatment, the hunger will help overcome their shyness, and they will eat and mingle easily with the other fish.

The optimum breeding temperature for this Gourami, as well as the other species, is about 79° F. At this higher temperature their color is more intense than at lower temperatures.

The Thick-Lipped Gourami, *Colisa labiosa*. Female is in front. (*Photo by Helmut Pinter*.)

The Striped Gourami, *Colisa fasciata*. Female in front. Note the great similarity between this and the above species, which are frequently confused. (*Photo by Helmut Pinter*.)

Dwarf Gourami (*Colisa lalia*) is a gentle member of the "bubble-nest builders."

Chocolate Gourami (*Sphaerichthys osphromenoides*) is a newer addition to the Gourami family. It is difficult to induce this fish to spawn and still more difficult to raise the young.

Other Gouramis are popular, too. The striped Gourami, *C. fasciata,* is also—incorrectly—called the "Giant Gourami," both names being attributed to the physical characteristics of the fish. This species has the general breeding habits of the family, and the female should be removed after spawning. The species is rather peaceful toward other fish, as is the entire group.

The Thick-lipped Gourami, *C. labiosa,* is halfway between the size of the Giant and the Dwarf, and not as colorful as either. Though its "lips" are not really very different from the other Gouramis, a careful comparison with other types will undoubtedly reveal some contrasts.

Three-spot Gourami
(*Trichogaster trichopterus*)

The Three-spot Gourami, *Trichogaster trichopterus,* may be a popularly misnamed species. Actually, the species has only two spots, large and dark, on its body. The third spot is generally considered to be the eye.

The Three-spot is not as peaceful as the other Gouramis and has been known to attack smaller fish. Though it also builds a bubble nest, it really does not need it since its eggs are lighter than water and float. The young, too, when they hatch out of the eggs, are very light and float on the surface of the water. The Three-spot and the Blue Gourami are identical except that the Blue Gourami has a hazy coat of whitish blue, which does not obscure the spots, however.

The Blue and Three-spot Gouramis, as well as the Pearl Gourami, which we shall mention presently, are well known for their hydra eating. Hydras are tiny pests with sharp, jagged tentacles which contain a potent venom. When a small fish comes into contact with their tentacles it is held fast and paralyzed, and then devoured. Hydras also have an appetite for Daphnia, which are more their own size. The writer has observed hydras that have

The Cosby strain of
Trichogaster trichopterus,
showing a male under a bubble
nest. (*Photo by Gerhard
Budich.*)

Hydras. These dreaded animals
easily trap and kill small fry.
The Pearl Gourami is used
in ridding a tank of hydras.
Note the whip-like tentacles
which ensnarl and stun small
fish. (*Courtesy General
Biological Supply House.*)

Kissing Gourami (*Helostoma temmincki*). It is easy to see how this fish got its name. The "kissing" is not a part of the Gourami's love technique, however.

Pearl Gourami (*Trichogaster leeri*).

had all their tentacles filled with paralyzed Daphnia, awaiting suitable appetite to ingest the unfortunate victims.

As can be understood, therefore, hydras are not welcome guests in the home aquarium. When they have infested the aquarium, about the only economical way to clear them out is to place a few Pearl Gouramis in the tank and let them stay hungry until they resort to eating hydras. After a time they get to relish these pests, and your hydra problem is solved.

Kissing Gourami
(*Helostoma temmincki*)

A very interesting Gourami is the Kissing Gourami, *Helostoma temmincki,* so named for the unusual shape of its mouth when eating or sucking debris from the sides of the tank. Kissing Gouramis seem to delight in sucking up debris on the bottom of the tank, ingesting whatever digestible matter it may contain. This Gourami is reputed to be an excellent algae eater, though the author is rather skeptical about this claim. Sometimes two Kissing Gouramis will come together with their puckered lips and actually kiss each other. This is probably not an act of love, in the sense that it is not part of a reproductive process or mating technique. In their native habitat, they run up to a foot long, though the average aquarium size is usually 5 to 6 inches. The larger the fish, the more dangerous.

Pearl Gourami
(*Trichogaster leeri*)

The *T. leeri,* or Pearl Gourami, is one of the most beautiful of the Gourami family. Reaching a length of 3 to 4 inches, it is one of the most peaceful and delightful fish to be added to a community tank. In breeding, the *T. leeri* develops a brilliant red hue. The eggs are lighter than water, and when the female is embraced under the bubble nest by the male, between thirty-five and a hundred eggs float up into the nest. Spawns sometimes reach into the thousands. The writer has been quite successful in raising *T. leeri* commercially in 100-gallon wooden-frame tanks.

The Pearl Gourami will spawn continuously during the summer months. If adequately fed, they will not eat their young and eggs. The whole secret in raising Gouramis is the feeding of the young. They should be fed four or five times a day at the minimum, with as much as they will take. A close look at their bellies, which should be like miniature balloons, will give ample indication of the success you are going to have. The young fish should be supplied with a profuse infusion. They should also receive egg yolk from the time they are free-swimming. To prepare this food, remove a piece of yolk from a hard-boiled egg. Wrap this piece of yolk in a clean white handkerchief and place it in warm water for a few seconds, then squeeze the yolk through the handkerchief and stir it into the water. Keep doing this until the water is a bright yellow. Feed it to the young fish through an eyedropper. (This egg suspension will keep in the refrigerator for a week, so the whole yolk of an egg may be prepared at one time.) The yolk makes a very desirable food since it does not sink as rapidly as regular dry food. After the first week, the young may be fed very fine, dry, powdered fish food, and after two weeks they should be fed brine shrimp with the egg suspension. Heavier foods may also be tried. The writer has been successful in raising the *T. leeri* up to maturity in nine months by a sole diet of egg and dried food.

Adult *T. leeri* relish Daphnia and Tubifex and are also dependent on floating foods. They should be supplied with these constantly.

Cichlids

Another large group of egg-laying fish is the family Cichlidae. These are characterized by having only a single opening to the nostril on either side of their heads, between the eyes and mouth.

Blue Acara (*Aequidens pulcher*), a Cichlid from Panama and Colombia, is an easy fish to spawn and very prolific.

The nostrils in most other fish are U-shaped tubes, with two openings to the exterior. (In neither the Cichlids nor most other fish do the nostrils communicate with the mouth or throat, being employed only in smelling and not breathing.)

The Cichlids vary so, both in appearance and in habits, that they would seem not to belong to the same family. Anyone who has seen the Angel Fish and the Egyptian Mouthbreeder will realize how different a Cichlid may look, and anyone who has bred these species knows how diverse are their breeding habits.

A discussion of those characteristics common to all but the exceptional few, however, will serve well as a general introduction to the care of the Cichlids as a group. The Cichlid is the largest type of fish that is normally kept in the home aquarium, but because of its size and temperament it is not too desirable for the community tank; its other characteristics more than make up for this temperament, however.

Breeding pairs of Cichlids are very hard to buy satisfactorily. Not only are the fish difficult to mate, but should a mated pair be purchased from a reputable dealer, there is no guarantee that they will breed again in strange surroundings. The best way to breed Cichlids is to plan your breeding in advance and prepare your own breeders. Most Cichlids are very inexpensive and readily available before they reach sizes over 2 inches. It is wise to purchase six to ten small Cichlids and place them in a large community tank to mature. When maturation has been reached, the fish will tend to pair off, one fish (usually the male) chasing after another particular fish (usually the female). When such is the case, it is easy to separate the two fish into a 10-gallon tank of their own and prepare to breed them. This method is probably the best way to breed a certain species of fish, but may be unsatisfactory owing to the time wasted in the maturation process. Most people contend that they would rather spend ten dollars for a mated pair of Cichlids than spend ten dollars on the live food necessary to bring the fish to a rapid maturation and seasoning. This is fine, except that after you have spent the money for the mated pair, there is no reward for you if the fish will not reproduce, and you are stuck with a pair of vicious fish that are valueless for your original purpose. So, if possible, try to obtain a group of small Cichlids and bring them to sexual maturation in your own tank. The thrill of knowing that you are entirely responsible for the brood, as well as the fact that you are not gambling with nature, more than makes up for the time consumed in maturation.

The selection of the mate is a serious process. Just as other types of living creatures have definite patterns of mating, so do fish. Birds sometimes fight over a mate, and the male often may attack and damage the female in trying to force his attentions upon her. A male pigeon, for instance, may peck a female's head until it is bloody in his attempt to "win" her. A similar occurrence is to be found with this most intelligent fish, the Cichlid. The male Cichlid will attack the female Cichlid much in the manner that

Cichlids perform a "marriage ritual" of locking jaws prior to spawning. Should one fish lose out, the pair should be separated and further conditioned until they are again up to full vigor and health.

the *Betta* will attack his mate. Plants will be torn up by the roots, and any small ornament is sure to be displaced as the battle between male and female persists. As it is not infrequent that the two fish will lock their strong jaws and roll over and over on the bottom of the tank, it is not advisable to have any sharp rocks or decorations on the floor of the aquarium. With some types of fish, this may continue for a few days, but others usually stop after six or eight hours. If the fish have been properly seasoned for this encounter, by being separated by a glass partition and being fed live food for a week or so before the mating, they usually proceed to mate and spawn with no trouble. But, should one be in better condition than the other, and should this superiority show in the love duel, then death is sure to be the reward of the weaker one. This may be nature's test for parenthood, but it is always wisest to prevent this mating fight, as the weaker fish invariably loses its life if it is allowed to occur. As is easily seen, then, it is usually best to have the fish of approximately the same size, though Cichlids differing an inch or more in length have been successfully bred.

Should this marriage test fail, that is, should one of the fish be stronger and start to overcome the other, then the fish should be separated, and new mates be provided for each after a further seasoning period. This second period should be longer than the first in order to give their wounds a chance to heal.

When a pair has finally been mated, they must be sure to have the proper "rooms" in which to breed. Several considerations must be taken into account in providing a favorable situation.

We know that the smallest breeding size of the average Cichlid is about 3 inches. Two of these make 6 inches. Since you anticipate a nice fight, several hundred (more or less) young, and possibly many holes being dug in the sand on the bottom, the minimum requirement would be a 10-gallon tank. The water should be well aged and at about 78° F.; plants are not necessary and should be omitted, except where mentioned for specific fish.

Prior to mating, the fish usually dig holes in the sand on the bottom of the tank; they grab a mouthful of sand and blow it a few inches away, until, by repeating this process many times, they produce a hole. Then they may move to another location and start the process all over again.

Their next step is to find a suitable place to protect their eggs. Since the eggs are adhesive and small, the parents must find a very clean, satisfactory depository. This is usually a flat, smooth stone. Once the stone has been selected, they scrub it with their mouths until every speck of debris or algae has been removed and the rock is spotless. As the Cichlids seem to prefer a light-colored stone, a piece of light slate or quartz is suitable. It should be at least 3 inches square, though its edges need not be uniform.

Now everything is in readiness for spawning. The fish develop a tube that projects from the anal region like a nipple; this is a sure signal that they are ready to spawn. The tube gets to be about three-eighths of an inch in most types of Cichlids. It is through this tube that the female drops her eggs and that the male emits his sperm to fertilize the eggs. After spawning, the tube slowly recedes into the body of the adult fish; this usually takes about five days to a week.

Now that the eggs are on the clean rock, fertilized by the male,

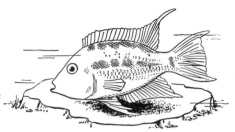

Most Cichlids prefer to spawn on a flat, hard surface like a rock. A piece of slate is usually best.

they are ready to be incubated. This incubation period observed by the Cichlids is analogous to that of the pigeon or the chicken. The eggs need oxygen to carry on life processes. If the water in the tank is still and the eggs are very compact (there may be several hundred eggs in a 3-inch square), it is easily seen that they do not receive much oxygen from the water immediately surrounding them. Undoubtedly it is for this reason that one of the parents stays above the eggs and fans them with its fins, gently forcing water over the eggs. It is a good thing that the eggs are sticky or they would be scattered all over the tank by this operation. Fanning the eggs probably has other purposes besides getting oxygen into the range of the eggs; wastes from the young embryos are diluted more quickly into the water, and the temperature is kept rather constant throughout the area by the greater circulation. This is an important part of the reproductive cycle of the Cichlid. After carefully fanning the eggs for a few hours, the parents make sure that none have been attacked by fungus. If they spot any that have been attacked, they eat them. Sometimes they eat the rest as well, but such is usually not the case. It has been said that they can exercise judgment as to whether or not their spawn are up to par, and if they are not, they eat them. But as far as the writer knows, there are no scientific data to support this theory.

As soon as the young are about to hatch, after about five days, the parents take them into their mouths and move them to one of the depressions they have dug in the sand. During the many trips that may be needed to carry them all, one of the parents is always awaiting the arrival of the other at one of the destinations, to make sure that they never lose all their young at one time. After a day or so, the young seem continually to be moved from one hole to the next, in the same careful way, always being guarded by their parents. Should any other fish venture near their hole, the parents either eat their young or fight the aggressor.

So far as can be determined, this daily moving is to provide the young, when they are old enough to eat, with fresh feeding grounds. The holes also provide good protection against possible enemies and an easy way for the parents to keep their brood concentrated in one small area. Any too venturesome young fish, straying beyond the confines of its "nursery," is quickly snapped up by one of the parents and spat back into the hole.

Cichlids, as a whole, are very good parents, and many of them may be left with their growing young. It may be wise, however, to remove the parents as soon as the young are free-swimming, since they are not essential to their young after they reach this size, and one never knows when a temperamental fish will start to eat its own offspring.

Among average aquarists, Cichlids are usually unpopular for their size and because they eat small fish with no concern at all. Some of these Cichlids get to be very nasty, and for that reason may require a separate tank for themselves. The famed *Astronotus ocellatus,* which gets to be very large (close to a foot long), must be fed live food constantly in the form of small fish (such as Guppies, Mollies, etc.), earthworms, chunks of meat, or pieces of shrimp. There are few, if any, tropical fish that may be kept safely in the same tank as *Astronotus.*

There is one important rule in dealing with Cichlids: *Give them plenty of room.* A pair of Cichlids should not be kept in a tank smaller than 10 gallons.

The breeding habits of the Cichlids, as you have seen, are very interesting. As the foregoing discussion has of necessity been general, we shall now progress to more specific discussions about the popular Cichlids, how to breed each group, and their peculiarities.

Certain of the Cichlids breed alike, but such fish as the Angel Fish (*Pterophyllum eimekei*), Egyptian Mouthbreeder (*Haplochromis multicolor*), and Jewel Fish (*Hemichromis bimaculatus*), though members of the same family, display different breeding habits. There is no reason to expect fish of the same family to breed exactly the same way; fish are classified according to physical characteristics, not according to breeding habits.

Acara
(*Cichlasoma festivum*)

The breeding habits of the Acara (*Cichlasoma festivum*) might be well worth investigation and thorough study, as the Acara is unique: it seldom gets larger than 3½ inches in length and is very peaceful for a Cichlid.

As mentioned previously (see p. 74 on the pairings of Cichlids) the best way to obtain a mated pair is to allow them to pair off by themselves. When you notice the peculiar antics of a pair of fish, remove them to a tank that has been prepared in advance for them. The tank should be unplanted but contain some types of dense vegetation. Any of the long, stiff-stemmed variety are good; place a rubber band about the bottom of a bunch and just drop it into the tank. Several inches of clean sand should be placed on the bottom of the tank, and a clean, light-colored, flat stone or small flowerpot should be placed on the sand. Next, the fish should be separated, as with the *Betta,* by a glass partition. This separation should continue until both fish are ready for the actual process of spawning. While the fish are thus separated, they must continually be fed freeze-dried food—any of the usual kinds are good, Daphnia, Tubifex, or brine shrimp probably being about the best.

When both fish show full color—for the Acara this is a deep

Cichlasoma festivum is a beautiful and peaceful Cichlid. Though this fish has been successfully spawned, it is still a difficult trick. The *festivum* is rather shy and hides quite frequently.

gray, with a long band of black running from the mouth, through the eye, across the back to the tip of the dorsal fin—they may be allowed to get together by a removal of the glass partition. As soon as the partition is removed, the fish will slyly investigate this new condition, hardly paying any attention to each other. This is in direct contrast to the actions of the *Bettas,* who, even when separated, dash against the glass partition in a vain attempt to reach the other fish.

After making sure that there are no enemies, the fish methodically go about tearing up any planted vegetation, as if making sure that no evil lurks in darkened corners. Next comes a process of much interest. The fish face each other and lock jaws, twisting and turning, rolling and milling, all over the tank. Again, be sure that there are no sharp edges upon which the fish may cut themselves. This test of strength may be repeated several times during a period of a few hours. Everything will be all right if neither fish gets "cold feet" and runs away from the other when approached. Should such be the case, the fish must be separated immediately or the coward is sure to meet its death. You may try to recondition the fish, but the chances of succeeding on the second try are definitely less than on the first. For this reason you must be sure that the fish are ready for mating before you separate them by the glass partition.

Should this "wrestling" period be consummated successfully, they will then proceed to dig holes in the sand. This interesting process may take several days, the fish gobbling a mouthful of sand and blowing it away from the hole. Next, the fish start chewing and scraping at every surface of the stone you have placed on the sand, to ensure maximum cleanliness. This action reminds one of the Molly scraping algae from the sides of the aquarium. The painstaking care with which this rock is prepared for the deposit of the eggs makes human cleanliness and meticulousness seem rather shoddy.

You can be quite sure that the pair will spawn in a very short time when both fish develop a short tube from the anal region. This tube (called an "ovipositor" in the female) reaches a length of about three-eighths of an inch immediately before spawning, though the size is usually proportional to the size of the fish. The Acara usually spawns about a day and a half after the appearance of this tube. During this entire process, the male and female fish stay very close to each other, usually in one of the holes they have previously dug.

When all is in readiness, the female approaches the selected rock and deposits a few eggs on it from her ovipositor; this may be repeated many times until an area of 3 square inches is covered with eggs; the male immediately follows and fertilizes the sticky eggs by squirting his sperm on them. After four or five hours, the fish are usually finished spawning, and begin to fan the eggs. Fanning is accomplished by the male or female staying directly above the mass of eggs and moving its pectoral and caudal fins unceasingly. When one fish gets tired, the other takes its place. The reasons for this fanning process may be threefold. First, by constant circulation, the temperature of the water is kept rather constant—80° F. is best—which undoubtedly helps the development of the eggs. Next, the circulation may help prevent bacteria or fungus from lodging on the infertile eggs and "rotting" them. Third, the fanning may keep fresh oxygenated water constantly over the eggs, avoiding a concentration of carbon dioxide and other wastes.

After four days at 80° F., the eggs start to hatch. At this time the fish start to move the young, mouthful by mouthful, to one of the holes which one fish has dug while the other was fanning the eggs. Sometimes a lazy pair will just use the holes that were dug before actual spawning took place. The transfer of the young is well organized. The rock is protected by one of the fish while the other protects the hole into which the young are being transferred. The rock protector gets a mouthful of young, signals the other fish (how this is done is not known, but they do face each other for a second or so before moving), and they quickly exchange places. The new mouthful of young is deposited with the others in the hole, and the fish repeat the process. This is kept up until all the fish are removed from the rock. Any infertile eggs which have started to rot are eaten by one of the fish. The young are then continually moved from hole to hole, being scrubbed by their trip in the parents' mouth. Do not misinterpret this as an act of eating. Now the young should be left alone with the parents; if the parents are disturbed or too badly frightend by an intruder, they *will* eat their litter right up.

For a week or so after hatching, the fish may be noticed to possess a yolk sac. This yolk sac contains food for the embryo fish

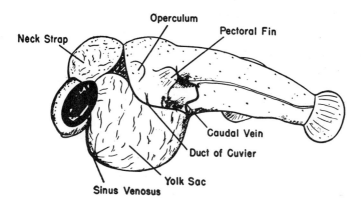

This newborn fish is a young egglayer. Note the yolk sac. All fish develop from eggs. Live bearers (such as the Platy), develop their eggs internally, giving birth to live young.

as well as a ration for a short time after it hatches. However, this sac is soon absorbed, and food must be provided for the young. Infusoria are the best. The larger types of paramecia, amoebae, and rotifers are good for the first few weeks; then quantities of sifted Daphnia or brine shrimp must be supplied. Microworms may also be used.

During this entire breeding process, the older fish must constantly be fed live food (Gordon's formula, p. 188, is also recommended). This holds true of all the Cichlids except the Egyptian Mouthbreeder.

The parents may be left with their young as long as you wish. During the first few days the young are definitely dependent on their parents, but after a week or so the parents may be moved —at the aesthetic expense of not being able to be watched swimming with their brood.

Cichlids may be bred again six weeks after they are removed from their brood, though breeding them too often is not advisable, as they tend to lose interest in their successive broods.

Aequidens portalegrensis

The Portalegrensis is a very popular fish and one that should be able to be successfully bred by whoever tries. It follows the breeding habits of the Cichlids, though offering more tolerance to critical conditions. The Ports usually can stand overcrowding, disturbances, and poor breeding conditions, while other Cichlids can't.

Aequidens portalegrensis are about 4 inches at breeding size, usually getting larger after a few successful breedings. They are very shy, and when introduced into a new aquarium, usually stay well hidden in some obscure corner of the tank. Often they will refuse the most enticing foods for a few days, preferring to stay in complete seclusion. Even if they are the sole members of the tank and are left undisturbed, there is little chance that they will be very active for the first few days. But, as always, their hunger pains eventually change their attitude, and they finally realize that their keeper is only interested in their welfare.

Sex may be easily determined by observing the shape of the anal fin, the male's being the more pointed and flowing, while the female's is shorter and rounded. In order to see this difference easily, you must compare the two fish together. After a little practice, you will be able to distinguish the males from the females easily.

Care should be taken to get fish of approximately the same size if you intend to breed them. One interesting fact about this fish is that when a pair have once spawned, they usually stay mated forever. This was observed under the following conditions: out of a brood of twenty *A. portalegrensis* raised together, six pairs developed. The fish were matured in a community tank all together, but were removed, pair by pair, to spawn in a separate tank. When their spawning was over, they were again placed in the community tank with the other Ports. Subsequent spawning always took place with the original mates. Never did any fish try to intercede with another's mate. This is an unusual characteristic for a fish to possess, since in so many cases more than one male is used for mating.

Jewel Fish
(*Hemichromis bimaculatus*)

The viciousness of certain fish makes them undesirable for the home aquarist. But if the fish has a nearly unparalleled beauty of color, some people will put up with its savage idiosyncrasies. Such is the case with the Jewel Fish (*Hemichromis bimaculatus*), which is one of the most savage aquarium fish.

Breeding must be carefully supervised. In addition to the material suggested in the general discussion of the preparation of a tank, some very dense foliage must be added, the best being large clumps of Elodea. The necessity for such foliage is easily seen when you realize that the Jewel Fish is probably the most active, sexually, of the Cichlids during the spawning interlude. Should one of the fish show the slightest signs of weakness, the other would immediately rip it to pieces; such dense foliage will help save the fish from such an end.

In addition to the plants, a good suggestion has been made, by A. N. Solberg and F. J. Brinley of North Dakota State University, that a flowerpot be placed in the tank for the purpose of egg deposition.

The Jewel Fish are quite beautiful when in breeding colors. They are bred the same way as the Acara and *A. portalegrensis*. Some authors suggest the use of the mature eggs of the *Hemichromis* for embryological studies. The previously mentioned authors, Solberg and Brinley, have done some serious work on the embryological development of the fish, and have found that heart action begins about thirty-six hours after fertilization, and that forty-eight hours after fertilization the embryo bursts from its

Jewel Fish (*Hemichromis bimaculatus*) attacking an inquisitive finger that is heading for its spawn on the rock. The fish will attack any fish or object that threatens the eggs or young.

containing membrane by a violent swish of its tail and moves away. They state that the yolk is absorbed after seven days, and advise that at this time, when the jaws become movable, the young Jewels should be fed protozoa.

Other fish which have the same breeding habits as the Acara, *A. portalegrensis,* and *H. bimaculatus* are as follows:

HERICHTHYS CYANOGUTTATUS—commonly called the "Texas Cichlid"; in Texas, they call it a "Perch." These fish are usually caught and eaten by the Mexicans and poor whites in and around the Rio Grande. While on a visit to San Antonio, the author saw them swimming in the river which flows right through the heart of town. They run to about 8 inches and are rather pretty, being covered with pearl-like speckles. They should be kept by themselves in a large tank.

CICHLASOMA MEEKI—commonly called the "Firemouth Cichlid." The Firemouth is so named because of the brilliant red color it develops on the underside of its body, from the base of the tail to the mouth. Sex is distinguished by the shape and size of the anal fin. A 10-gallon tank is necessary for the Firemouths, as they sometimes get to be 6 inches long and need room to spawn. They breed very much the same as other fish, except that it is advisable to have a piece of slate for them to spawn on; because if you have a slate-bottom tank and do not place in a rock, they will dig through the sand and spawn on the bottom. The size of the slate should be about 5 by 10 inches. Thickness is of no consequence.

CICHLASOMA BIOCELLATUM—commonly called the "Jack Dempsey" because of its ferociousness. It is truly a beautiful fish, always displaying magnificent colors, which tend not to change much and are almost permanent. The Jack Dempsey can stand the normal fluctuation of temperature from 60° to 90° F. without any trouble, though the color is at its best around 82° F.

After a year, the fish may reach 4 inches in length, usually getting larger and more colorful as it gets older. It breeds as we would expect any of the Cichlids to breed and is an exceptionally good parent, though it must not be disturbed too frequently.

A pair of Dempseys breed best when they are kept in a 20-gallon tank by themselves. They may be kept with their young and usually take excellent care of them.

They should be fed on live food and Gordon's formula (see p. 188).

CICHLASOMA SEVERUM—This fish is not too commonly found in the home aquarium, owing to its timidity and the difficulties that arise when trying to breed it. The slightest noise or ripple on the water frightens these fish enough to make them lose their color; even the introduction of food into the water makes them nervous. It takes weeks before they will act normally in a strange tank, so for this reason you will do best by keeping them in a tank by themselves.

This fish grows little larger than 5 inches long and will get along nicely in a 10- or 12-gallon aquarium. Conditioning before mating is very important, and they should be fed live food or chopped earthworms for a few weeks before trying to spawn them. They will show little color at temperatures below 78° F. The optimum breeding temperature is about 80° F. Sex may be determined by a comparison of the anal fins. As always, the male fin is longer and more pointed. The male is also more highly colored, being covered during high color with rows of parallel dots. The female has at times faded vertical bands, though in a matter of seconds, if frightened she may lose every bit of color she previously had.

ETROPLUS MACULATUS—commonly called the "Orange Chromide," is similar to *C. severum* in that it, too, is a very shy and timid fish. Add to this timidity its refusal to eat several types of dry foods and you have an idea why it is so difficult to breed. It is a small fish for a Cichlid, seldom getting larger than 3 inches. As sex is rather difficult to distinguish, and mated pairs are hard to obtain, the group and pairing plan is about the only way to get a decently mated pair. This method is further advantageous in that the Orange Chromide will breed in a community tank, as long as the other fish are not too large. The mother fish will usually tend the young while the father tries to keep strangers away from them.

The fish are peculiar in that they will spawn on the top part of the inside of a flowerpot, or on the underside of the slate if the slate is laid against the side of the tank rather than being placed flat against the sand. They are a nice fish to keep in the community tank because of their size and breeding habits.

AEQUIDENS MARONII—commonly called the "Keyhole Fish" because of the dark region near its lower quarter which takes the shape of a keyhole. The reason for the name *maronii* is simple: the fish was originally found in the Maroni River in Venezuela. This fish should be very popular, but for some reason it is not. Keyhole Cichlids are very mild mannered and usually will not

Orange Chromide (*Etroplus maculatus*), a beautiful Cichlid from India, is quite easily spawned.

attack any smaller fish without provocation. They are fairly timid and lose their color when frightened. Sex is easily determined by a comparison of the anal fins of the male and female, the male's fin being much longer and more pointed.

The Keyhole Cichlids are good parents and may be bred easily by the amateur if the proper conditioning precautions are followed. They thrive well on all types of live food and seem to relish the Gordon preparation (p. 188) in between feedings of live food.

ASTRONOTUS OCELLATUS—commonly called by its full Latin name. Anyone owning a mated pair of these fish paid over seventy-five dollars for them, and anyone who believes he can breed them and successfully rear the young knows enough about fish not to rely upon popular names. They are vicious, large (up to a foot in length), and very difficult to breed. Though in relatively rare instances they have been successfully bred, they probably did their spawning alone in a 100-gallon tank, or larger. This will usually put them out of reach of the ordinary fancier. A 100-gallon tank filled with water weighs close to half a ton, and not many homes have floors than can stand such a concentrated weight.

The *A. ocellatus* is pugnacious looking, and, in character with its looks, it makes short work of any fish smaller than 3 inches, and has been known to attack larger fish. Sometimes young are available, but as they grow they will eat larger and larger fish.

If they do spawn, their eggs must be removed and hatched in a large 35-gallon tank by themselves.

The Red Devils
(*Cichlasoma erythraeum* and *Cichlasoma dovii*)

Late in 1964 these monsters among aquarium fishes were introduced to hobbyists. Some of them are so big that they even make a grown Oscar look small, and if you don't have a tank that's really big, forget about them! Home waters are in several parts of Central America, Costa Rica and Nicaragua being two of the possibilities mentioned. They vary greatly in color as well as shape, some of them being pure white and others red all over, some with black markings on fins and the mouth. Some have large rubbery lips that come to a point and remind one of some of the salt-water Wrasse species.

Egyptian Mouthbreeder
(*Haplochromis multicolor*)

The Egyptian Mouthbreeder is truly a fish to catch the eye. Not only is it very neatly colored, but its breeding habits are most unusual. The habits of breeding are similar to those of the other

Velvet Cichlid (*Astronotus ocellatus*) is a vicious fish that grows to over a foot long. It breeds on occasion but mated pairs are very expensive when purchased.

Young Astronotus look quite different from their parents. Even when only an inch long they will attack and eat Guppies one-half inch long.

Cichlids only in that a hole made by the fish for itself—usually by fanning the sand—is used for depositing the eggs. The male entices the female over the hole and she drops a few eggs into it; they are then quickly fertilized by the male. However, following this, the process is quite different from that of the other Cichlids. As soon as fertilization takes place, the female swoops down and gathers up the fertile eggs in her mouth. She may continue to do this for some time, but as soon as her mouth is full, she will no longer go near the hole. Sometimes this irritates the male and he will nip at her; the female, with her mouthful of eggs, is helpless to fight back, and unless the merciful intervention of the aquarium manager saves her, she may die with her brood still in her mouth. For this reason, it seems wise to remove the male as soon as possible after the female exhibits signs of leaving her position over the hole.

Day after day, the female keeps her eggs in her mouth, sucking water in over them through her mouth and blowing it out of her gills. She will steadily refuse the most tasty morsels offered her, never daring to take anything into her oral cavity. This refusal to eat may last as long as two weeks, during which time the young fish hatch and live off their yolk sacs. The mother may at times allow her brood to swim around her out of her mouth, but at the slightest noise or disturbance, she will open her mouth and the young will swim directly in. During this time, the female fish may appear to lose all her flesh; she will get very thin and emaciated, and her eyes will seem to bulge from their sockets. So strong is this mother's instinct, however, that, as hungry as she is, she would rather starve to death than eat her own young. After about two weeks, the young are too large to be able to fit into the mouth of their mother, so they take off on their own, searching for the protozoa or Infusoria that should be placed in the tank for them.

One odd thing about the Egyptian Mouthbreeders is that they will attack and kill any of the swiftly swimming fish that may be present in their mating tank. This is undoubtedly a precaution they take, fearing that a fast-moving fish might swoop down upon their brood before they get a chance to seek refuge in their mother's mouth.

It should be mentioned that no amount of physical manipulation will persuade the female to release her young before they are of the proper size. She will keep her mouth locked even when lifted from the tank.

After she has served her purpose, the mother fish should be put in a small tank alone for a few days so she can regain her health without being bothered by stronger fish attacking her. She should be fed small amounts of Daphnia or Tubifex at frequent intervals, but not too much at once as she may become ill.

The optimum temperature for the breeding of the young and the mating of the parents is about 78° F. The young should be fed live food as often as possible for quick maturation.

Sex in these fish is easily discernible by the larger head of the female and the more brightly colored anal fin of the male during high color.

The Nyasa Cichlids
(*Pseudotropheus* and
Labeotropheus species)

Every time the hobbyists of the world become jaded and say that there is nothing new to be seen among fishes, it seems that someone comes along with the news that a new source has been found and there is a new set of tongue-twisting names to learn and fishes to admire. In 1965 collectors found a new supply of fishes in Lake Nyasa, in the eastern part of Africa. Now a strange part of many of these African lakes is that they harbor a fish life that is found nowhere else in the world except in that particular lake.

A male *Pseudotropheus auratus* from Nyasa Lake (Malawi).

The Golden Nyasa Cichlid
(*Pseudotropheus auratus*)

One of the most beautiful of the newcomers from Lake Nyasa is this one, which is already creating a bit of a furor among hobbyists. It was quickly established that this was a mouthbreeding species, but so scrappy in disposition that two males should never be kept together, unless the tank is very large and each can lay claim to a certain part of the tank for himself. They spawn like the other mouthbreeding Cichlids, the female carrying the eggs in her mouth for two weeks. Unlike the other mouthbreeders, these have been observed to spit out the eggs on occasion and eat a hearty meal. At this time the eggs can be siphoned out and allowed to hatch, and there are reports that this has been done successfully. But we still have much to learn about this beauty.

A male *Pseudotropheus zebra* . Note the egg-shaped spots in his anal fin.

The Zebra Nyasa Cichlid
(*Pseudotropheus zebra*)

This is another of the new ones from Lake Nyasa. Body color is blue, with a number of vertical black bars. The male's anal fin has a group of interesting orange spots, which have an intriguing story, as have those on some of the other mouthbreeding species.

The male stands by while the female lays her eggs in a depression in the bottom and then picks them up in her mouth. Then he spreads out his anal fin with those orange spots in front of her. The spots look like eggs to her, and she picks at them vigorously while at the same time the male is emitting sperm, which gets to all the eggs and fertilizes them.

No doubt we will soon be hearing about this species spawning in captivity.

The Trewavas Nyasa Cichild
(*Labeotropheus trewavasae*)

So differently colored are the male and female of this species that
it was at first thought they were two different species. The male
has a blue body with a number of dark vertical stripes and a
bright red dorsal fin, while the female is mottled brown all over,
with darker markings and tiny blue spots. Both have an odd,
underslung mouth. This is probably a mouthbreeding species like
the others, but we have not heard any spawning reports as yet.

The Compressed Cichlid
(*Lamprologus compressiceps*)

This is one of the many Cichlids which are found in Lake Tanganyika and, it seems, nowhere else. They have a very thin body
which lets them slip in among the clefts of the rocks. The natives
collect them by diving to a depth of about 60 feet and feeling
among the rock clefts for them. The dorsal fin spines are very
sharp and cause an unpleasant itching if the skin is pierced, so if
you ever get to own one, handle it with care!

The Lemon Cichlid
(*Lamprologus leleupi*)

This little rarity comes from the home of many Cichlid species,
Lake Tanganyika. It gets to be only 4 inches in length, and is not
hard to keep if given living foods and water which is definitely
alkaline. They have been spawned, and breed like the usual
Cichlid species, using a flowerpot for the eggs which hatch in
three days. They are easily raised with the standard procedure.

Large Mouthbreeder (*Tilapia macrocephala*). This is the usual appearance of many Tilapia.

Large Mouthbreeder
(*Tilapia macrocephala*)

This fish is closely related to the Egyptian Mouthbreeder, except for the curious fact that the male is the "mother" in this case. It is the male that assumes the responsibility for carrying the young, and for this reason, after spawning, the female should be removed. Sex is quite easily determined by the color of the gill cover: in males this is lemon yellow; in females it is dull red—actually translucent, the gills showing through and giving the reddish color.

Breeding temperatures and habits are the same, except that the Large Mouthbreeders should be fed large amounts of Gordon's formula (see p. 188) with every feeding of live food. They sometimes prefer the formula to the live food, perhaps because there is more of it available for them.

This species is much gentler than the Egyptian. They will not attack any of the smaller fish as *H. multicolor* will, even though at their 6-inch size they are 3 inches larger than the Egyptian.

Angel Fish
(*Pterophyllum eimekei*)

The present "King of the Cichlids" bears little resemblance to members of his own tribe, but looks more like one of the salt-water Angel Fish, to which he is not at all closely related, but from which he derives his popular name. There has been much debate about which is the true *scalare* of the genus *Pterophyllum;* some experts claim that *Pterophyllum scalare* is very rarely imported and that none exist in captivity at present, and that the species *P. eimekei* is what is now usually called the *"scalare."* It would be rather senseless to present an argument here, as both fish have practically the same physical appearance and essentially the

Angel Fish (*Pterophyllum eimekei*), a truly elegant fish, not too difficult to breed. It is very difficult, however, to differentiate between the two sexes.

same breeding habits. The fish here described will be, for all intents and purposes, the *scalare,* either *P. scalare* or *P. eimekei.*

The Angel Fish, timid, temperamental, and delicate as it is, is probably the most popular egg-laying fish, comparable to *Betta splendens.* The interesting complexities of spawning and the intriguing techniques for rearing the young present a worthy challenge to the advanced aquarist. Many people have successfully bred the Angel, but it seems that no two people used the same techniques.

A Veiled Angel Fish with very good fin development. (*Photo by Dr. Herbert R. Axelrod.*)

A Black Lace Angel Fish. (*Photo by Louise Van der Meid.*)

A rarity: half of this Angel Fish's body is almost completely black. (*Photo by G. J. M. Timmerman.*)

Let us take a close look at a sensible approach to the breeding of the Angel Fish.

Since in the Angel Fish the two sexes are practically indistinguishable, the only way to get a mated pair is to use the group pairing method, allowing the fish to pair off by mutual attraction, or else to purchase a pair that has been successfully bred by another aquarist. Such breeding pairs are rather expensive, usually selling for not less than ten dollars per pair, whereas young Angels may be selected for less than fifty cents each. The size of breeding pairs varies from one pair to the next, the usual size being about 3 to 4 inches. The true *P. scalare* may get as large as 6 inches in an outdoor pond; the smaller *P. eimekei* usually is only about 5 inches. The young grow rapidly when reared on live food and Gordon's formula (see p. 188). Their attractiveness adds greatly to the appearance of the community tank, as they tend to swim in groups when kept in a large tank. They may be safely allowed to grow to breeding size without your having to worry about them attacking any fish larger than a Guppy. As there is little food better for the Angels than the newborn Guppy, it is usually a good idea to place them in a tank with a dozen or so Guppies so they may benefit from the constant source of live food. When the fish get very temperamental and refuse all types of food, they will usually accept Guppies. The same is true for a great many of the Cichlids which show signs of being too timid or afraid to eat.

When you have a breeding pair of Angels, your next step is to put them into a large, well-planted tank of their own. The reason for the dense foliage is twofold. First, since the Angel is, as previously mentioned, very timid and gets disturbed at the slightest provocation, the more vegetation there is, the more secure the fish will feel. The shadows and hiding places offered by the plants seem to instill confidence in the Angel. The other important reason is that the plants, especially Giant Vallisneria, Amazon Sword, and Giant Sagittaria, play a part in the spawning procedure of the Angels, the eggs of the fish many times being deposited on the stiff, rather broad leaves of the plants, which offer firm anchorage for the sticky eggs. On other occasions, the Angels may elect to deposit their eggs either on one side of the tank if it has some sort of paint on the outside, on the glass containing the heater or thermostat, or on the face of a piece of slate which has been left tilted against the side of the tank. It is easiest for the aquarist when the slate is used since the eggs can be removed without too much trouble. This removal is sometimes very necessary, because at the slightest provocation or alarm the eggs or newly hatched young may be gobbled down, out of the parents' fear for their welfare. It has been claimed many times that the parents eat their brood out of sheer dislike for the responsibility placed upon them, but there is little reason for such a theory. There are many cases known where parents successfully spawned and reared brood after brood of young, and then suddenly ate up the next spawning. This has been explained by research, which has shown that there is only one variable in the successive spawnings, the pH of the water. (Angel Fish do best in slightly acid water [pH 6.8] and, if left alone, they tend to maintain a tank at that pH; several factors, however, must be controlled if the pH level is to be maintained at 6.8.) The logical supposition, then, would be that the young were dying because of an intolerable pH, and that the parents were eating them as they died. There is little doubt, however, that if the parents are frightened, they will also be stimulated to this destructiveness.

Although the parents may be left in with the young for the entire maturation, if the tank is large enough (35 gallons), it is wiser either to remove them, if they have spawned on the plants or glass, or to remove the slate, if they have spawned on that. The slate should be placed in a shallow tank of 4 inches of water, with a drop of methylene blue for each gallon of water to prevent fungus; it should be slightly tilted off the bottom so an aerator may be placed underneath it, allowing the bubbles to flow all around it, and hence causing the water to circulate. This takes the place of the parents' usual habit of taking the young in their mouths for a scrubbing every once in while.

The optimum breeding temperature for the Angel is about 80° F. Seasoning on live food—Daphnia and white worms are the best, next to young Guppies, of course—is of the utmost importance in preparing the Angels for spawning.

The young must have live protozoa or Infusoria on hand for their first meal. After a few days, they must be fed sifted Daphnia, brine shrimp, or microworms. Brine shrimp seem to be the best.

The key factors in working with Angels are cleanliness and the pH. The water can never be clean enough for the Angels; it is usually wise to have a reserve jug of seasoned water at the proper temperature in case a cloudiness develops in the breeding tank. This cloudiness is often caused by too strong an infusion, that is, too dense a culture of small protozoa, or the rotting of organic matter.

The manner in which parents care for their eggs, should they be allowed to remain with them, is really impressive. Their actions are generally the same as the other Cichlids, except that instead of transferring the young from hole to hole—though they may do this, too—in the sand, they usually transfer them from leaf to leaf, by the mouthful. Should one of the young fall free from the leaf, the ever-alert parent will be sure to catch him and return him, in one gentle blow, to his proper place on the leaf.

Angel Fish have been produced in several varieties, all from the original *Pterophyllum eimekei*. To Ludwig's Aquarium in Detroit goes the credit for being the first to produce an all-black Angel Fish strain. Good specimens are solid black in color, making a wonderful appearance in a well-planted aquarium.

The Veil Angel Fish was once found as a sport in a batch of normal youngsters by a German breeder. He kept breeding it back to others until he arrived at a preponderance of long-finned beauties. Of course, it had to happen that the Blacks and Veils were crossed and a magnificent Black Veil strain was produced.

Discus
(Symphysodon aequifasciata axelrodi)

The Discus is probably unknown to many beginning aquarists owing to its size, cost and temperament. The fact that young Discus cost upward of five dollars each gives an idea of how difficult they are to breed. A mated pair may cost over five hundred dollars. Although the acquisition of a mated pair may guarantee spawning, raising the spawn is another story. Many advanced aquarists have spent fortunes on all types of equipment for fancy techniques to help their spawn to survive, but very few have had success.

The breeding of the Discus is similar to that of the Angel Fish, but the Discus is much more delicate and temperamental than any fish that has been previously mentioned. About the only food it will take are Miracle freeze-dried Tubifex worms, white worms, fairy shrimp, and Daphnia, and these only sparingly. Many a Discus has been lost because it simply refused to eat. Again, live Guppies may be offered.

The main interest of these fish is their scintillating beauty and nearly perfect circular shape. They display beautiful colors when spawning, which may be quite frequent when they are in a tank by themselves. They range in size up to 6 inches, and a 25-gallon tank should be their minimum requirement. The tank should be densely planted at both ends, leaving the center free for them to display their natural beauty.

If you can afford to purchase a half dozen of these young and raise them to maturity—this is not too great a feat if they start eating right away—they will pair off by mutual attraction when the time is ripe. This is about the only sure way to get a mated pair from them, as sex is practically indistinguishable.

In the past few years the Discus has attained a much more popular position than it held in the days when it was first offered

The King and Prince of the Aquarium World—the Angel Fish and the
Discus (*Symphysodon discus*). The Discus is considered to be the most
difficult to spawn. A mated pair are practically impossible to buy. The Discus
is choosy about its diet and will usually accept only live food in the form
of small fish or fairy shrimp.

to awe-struck hobbyists and commanded astronomical prices.
Since then it was discovered that spawning them, while still not
an everyday thing, is not the near impossibility it was once considered to be, and every well-stocked hobbyist nowadays is very
likely to have a few.

Dr. Leonard P. Schultz, of the Smithsonian Institution in Washington, D.C., has divided the *Symphysodon* genus into several
species and subspecies. At present there are four: *Symphysodon
aequifasciata aequifasciata,* the Green Discus; *Symphysodon
aequifasciata axelrodi,* the Brown Discus; *Symphysodon aequifas-*

Discus spawn on a flat stone or glass surface, just like Angel Fish. When the young hatch and become free-swimming, they attach themselves to the sides of the parents, grazing off of the body slime. (*Photos by Gerhard Budich.*)

It is a pretty sight to watch the young change from one parent to the other.

Growth is rapid, and here you can see how the young are beginning to acquire the body shape of the parents.

The vertical bars show much more plainly on young specimens, as you can see on these three. Color is also beginning to show in the dorsal and anal fins.

ciata haraldi, the Blue Discus; and *Symphysodon discus,* the original Red Discus or Pompadour.

Breeding the various Discus species is exactly the same, and the best method to get a well-mated pair is to keep about a half-dozen growing ones together and let them pick their own mates. They should have a large tank, about 50 gallons or more, and when two are observed to get chummy and claim a portion of the tank as their property, the time has come to give them a tank of their own. This tank should have soft water, a temperature of about 82° F. and an acidity that measures pH 6.5. Planting should be heavy, to give the pair some retreats where privacy can be attained. As with Angel Fish, it is a good procedure to lean a slab of slate against one side of the tank. This is generally where the pair will spawn. Some breeders prefer to give them a large flowerpot with the open top down. Preferences by the fish vary, and a little trial is indicated. Just like Angel Fish, the pair will swim close alongside each other, the female laying the eggs and the male fertilizing them. Then they take turns fanning and mouthing the eggs, which hatch after two days. The youngsters become free-swimming two days later, at which time they attach themselves to the sides of one of the parents and "graze" there until the time comes to change to the other parent. This is the big difference in Discus breeding: the youngsters usually do not do at all well unless they get this slime as their first food. Perhaps someday an acceptable substitute will be found and the eggs can be hatched artificially as Angel Fish eggs are, eliminating the danger of being eaten.

It is a fascinating sight to watch the parents "trading" the youngsters. The one with the youngsters feeding on the sides will wait for the other to swim up, then with a quick motion the youngsters are left behind to find their new feeding spot. In about two weeks the youngsters can be "weaned" to newly hatched brine shrimp, and when they no longer feed on the parents' slime the parents can be moved to their own tank. Frequently they are ready to spawn again by this time.

Discus are very timid fish and are easily frightened. For this reason, they should not have their tank where there are frequent disturbances. Any fish that must be left with its young as Discus are would be very likely to become panicky and eat the eggs and young whenever frightened.

Apistogramma ramirezi, a Dwarf Cichlid. The first rays on the dorsal fin are longer on the male than on the female.
(*Photo by G. J. M. Timmerman.*)

Dwarf Cichlids

With a natural consideration for the aquarist, importers have long been looking for a fish as interesting as the Cichlid but much smaller and more peaceful. The problem was easily solved with the acquisition of the now popular Dwarf Cichlids. These Cichlids, the *Nannacara* and *Apistogramma,* were only recently offered to the aquarist. In this instance, the aquarist has been able to help the ichthyologist by relaying to him his observations of the fish, because when the Dwarf Cichlids were first offered for sale, very little was known about their breeding habits.

The main advantage the Dwarfs have over their larger relatives is their temperament. No Dwarf Cichlid will tear up plants or attack the other fish in the community tank. Most of the Dwarfs can be spawned in 5-gallon tanks, since they seldom measure more than 3 inches in length. Care of the breeding pair is the same as with the larger Cichlids, with the possible exception that both parents should be separated from the eggs as soon as they spawn. The Dwarf Cichlids are especially fond of eating their eggs. The frequency of spawning depends upon the environment, but normally should be at least once a month from April through October. These Dwarf Cichlids are peculiar in that the female alone cares for the eggs and young, driving away the male after spawning has been completed.

Apistogramma ramirezi

As a characteristic Dwarf Cichlid, and the most beautiful, let us examine the *Apistogramma ramirezi*. The Ramirezis measure between 2 and 2½ inches in length. They get rather rounded, a shape that seems to be common to all mature Dwarf Cichlids. When in color, they show all the hues and shades their distant relative the Discus possesses. The only drawback is that they are very shy and timid. At the slightest shadow or loud noise, they hide in the vegetation. Breeding color is normally prevalent most of the year, provided the fish are supplied continually with live food. They seem to be especially partial to Tubifex, though too much Tubifex is too rich a diet for any fish. It is better to feed Tubifex two or three times a week, with intermittent feedings of Gordon's formula (see p. 188), white worms, Daphnia, and fairy shrimp.

You may have either a few inches of sand (deeper than for other Cichlids) or no sand at all. On top of the sand, if you use it, there should be placed a few pieces of slate, about 2 or 3 inches square. These are the slates on which the fish will deposit their spawn. In one corner of the tank you should have some thick vegetation. If possible, keep the tank covered with paper so that shadows of people walking by will not disturb the fish.

The Ramirezi is bred similarly to the other Cichlids. A few males (the first three black rays on the dorsal fin are much longer than those of the female) should be placed in a 10-gallon tank with a few females. Natural selection should get at least one pair from three or four fish. As soon as the Ramirezis have paired off, you will note that the pair will stay much to themselves in a corner, keeping the other fish away. At this time remove all the unmated fish, leaving the pair to themselves.

If the fish are properly mated, they should show small white breeding tubes prior to spawning. Plenty of Tubifex should be left around the tank with the appearance of these tubes. When the fish have spawned, remove the slates to a tank—from 3 gallons upward, the larger the better—to which has been added one drop of methylene blue per gallon of water. The water need be only the same temperature as that from which they were removed, from 75° to 85° F.; the eggs hatch, in three days, at 80° F. Keep a light on the eggs at all times so the bluish dye will be decomposed—in about five days—and the water will again be transparent. The young fish should be supplied with Infusoria the first weeks. As soon as they are free-swimming, they should be given newly hatched brine shrimp and microworms, and should be kept on this live food for four weeks. At four weeks they will take Gordon's formula (p. 188). The young fish mature at six months.

One of the most beautiful Cichlids from the African continent is the *Pelmatochromis kribensis*. They do very well on the diet and care recommended for *Apistogramma ramirezi,* but seem to go one step further when it comes to hiding their eggs from sight.

A very useful thing in the spawning aquarium is an ordinary clay flowerpot, with a piece broken out of the rim. This is stood on its open end in such a manner that the fish can swim in and out of the broken-out opening. They soon learn to accept this as their "home," but one day you will notice that the male, which is more than twice the size of the little female, is ejected every

A pair of *Pelmatochromis kribensis*. Note the additional markings on the fins of the male. (*Photo by G. J. M. Timmerman.*)

time he tries to gain entrance. Take him out and put him into another tank when this happens, or you will have a male that may soon be badly beaten up. The female, who of course is guarding eggs, will put in an appearance in about a week's time, herding a brood of fry. This is a good time to take her out as well and leave the youngsters to their own devices. Many breeders prefer to leave the female in for a week or two, but there is the danger that at any time the young might be eaten.

All the *Nannacara* and *Apistogramma* should be treated the same way as the *A. ramirezi*. See the Appendix for more information on Dwarfs.

Chapter 4
Other Egg Layers

Characins

The Characins may frequently be recognized by the possession of an adipose fin, which is located on the back between the dorsal and caudal fins. Breeding of all the Characins is quite similar, with a few exceptions (when you have bred one you can usually breed them all). There are two or three very important points to follow, when breeding, that apply to all the Characins.

1. Remove parents after spawning.
2. Feed plenty of Daphnia during the spawning process.
3. Keep temperature at about 75° F.
4. Have tank more or less filled with Nitella.
5. Have plenty of Infusoria and brine shrimp handy for maturation of the young fry.
6. Have no snails in tank with egg layers. Snails eat the eggs.

For the sake of clarity, let us select one Characin to be representative of the whole family, and discuss its breeding habits carefully.

Of all the Characins, the most beautiful and difficult to breed is the Neon Tetra (*Paracheirodon innesi*).[1]

---

[1] The author feels that the following discussion is one of the most valuable in the book, as it took many years of research and has never been presented in any publication. The author would appreciate any comments on this approach to the breeding of the Neon. The few people who know about this method have been able to raise successfully about eighteen to twenty-five fish per spawning. Perhaps the reader has a simpler, and just as successful, method.

The longest a Neon will grow is 1½ inches, about the size of a large male Guppy, but much more colorful than the Guppy could ever be expected to be. Even if breeding is difficult, the Neons deserve a place of honor in every community tank because of their unique beauty. They are rather peaceful and very active, always swimming about at high speeds. (This speed decreases slightly when the fish is preparing to spawn, which is one way you may be able to predict to some extent when the female will be ready to drop.)

The breeding of the Neon requires complete understanding of the general characteristics of the fish. A long, flat, 20-gallon tank should be filled with 15 gallons of water (about three-fourths full). Leaving the center free, the bottom should be lined with an abundance of sterilized dense foliage, Nitella being the best. The sides of the tank should also be spread with this Nitella to a thickness of about 2 inches. Have no sand on the bottom of the tank, but do have a few pieces of old log or twigs in the open center portion. Arrange the twigs so there is a maximum area of undersurface free for the young to attach themselves.

The water that is placed in the tank must be specially prepared; the entire success of breeding depends upon the preparation of this water. The primary concern is to have the water bacteria-free. The best water to use is distilled water that has been thoroughly aerated. The aeration apparatus must be sterilized by boiling for twenty minutes before insertion into the tank. Remember to keep everything that goes into the tank sterile. The plants (*Nitella*) must be sterilized by a thorough treatment with salt and potassium permanganate. The tank itself should be sterilized by soaking for forty-eight hours with a very concentrated solution of salt and potassium permanganate. The twigs may be sterilized by boiling in water for twenty minutes. The glass cover plate for the tank must also be sterilized, and can be placed in the tank with the sterilizing solution. Allow the glass to dry in the air; if the solution was concentrated enough, there will be a salt deposit left on the glass plate when it has been dried. Next, drain the water

Blind Cave Fish (*Anoptichthys jordani*) has an interesting history. Found in La Cueva Chica, Mexico, much research on it was being done by Dr. C. M. Breder, Jr., and his staff at the American Museum of Natural History. Even without eyes the fish rarely hits rocks and has no difficulty finding food or spawning.

Neon Tetra (*Paracheirodon innesi*) is so colorful and beautiful that many fish exhibitions will not judge them against other fish. Very difficult to breed; many are therefore imported.

out of the tank and refill it with the sterile water (boiled for twenty minutes, then cooled); then aerate it for twenty-four hours.

The optimum temperature for the breeding of the Neon is 78° F. The best way to approach this temperature is with a thermostatically controlled heater that has a guiding light that shows when the heater is working. Sterilize this heater by boiling that part of the heater which will be submerged in the water. Steam the top, or wash it with alcohol.

When you have selected a very heavy female—she is easily recognized by her roundness, in comparison with the slim male— she may be placed for an hour in a solution of salt and potassium permanganate. If you use a net that has been used for other purposes, make sure it has been sterilized before using it to remove the female from the salt solution. Then put her in the tank when the temperature is about 74° F. (of course, the water in the tank from which she has been taken should be the same temperature).

Next, select the male and place him in a weaker solution of salt, and gradually raise the temperature in this solution to 78° F. At the same time, raise the temperature of the water in the breeding tank to 78° F., and place the male with the female. Then cover the entire tank with a large towel or sheet; this ensures a minimum amount of light and a minimum fluctuation of temperature.

The fish will need some sort of live or freeze-dried food, the best undoubtedly being grown brine shrimp. These brine shrimp are to be raised in a very strong salt solution. If you use a large-mouthed eye dropper, it will be easy to regulate the amount of food you drop in. Care must be taken to feed them enough to satisfy their hunger, but not to feed them more than they will eat. Spawning will take place, after a few days, when the male chases the female into the vegetation. The eggs are dropped at random while the female swims through the dense foliage, and fertilization is haphazard.

Head-and-Tail-Light (*Hemigrammus ocellifer*). Note the silvery appearance of the head and at the base of the tail.

Hemigrammus pulcher.

As soon as spawning is completed—if the female is very heavy it should not take more than forty-eight hours—remove the female. The female should be removed before the male, as she is the one that will eat the eggs; the male tries to protect the eggs by constantly chasing the female from them. The eggs are very small and practically colorless. They will hatch out in thirty-six hours and they may be seen clinging to the logs in the water. The young do not resemble anything at all. They are small and colorless, taking upward of four weeks before they show color. They should be fed on as pure a culture of Infusoria, preferably rotifers, as can be prepared; when four weeks old, they will take brine shrimp.

The pH of the water should be kept as close to 7.0 (neutral) as possible.

The Neon may have been an unfortunate selection to illustrate breeding generalities, but if anyone can reproduce Neons, he can breed any fish. In general, all Characins may be bred the same way as the Neon, with the omission of the sterilization processes. (Variations in conditions will be noted under the discussions of the individual fish.)

Cardinal Tetra
(*Cheirodon axelrodi*)

When the author brought this fish to the attention of the scientific and aquarium world, it immediately became a favorite and is now more popular than the Neon Tetra. Discovered in the Rio Negro, near Barcelos, Brazil, as well as near Puerto Gaitan, Colombia, this easy-to-keep beauty should make a valuable addition to the community aquarium. It is peaceful, very colorful, and eats all types of prepared and live foods. Females are heavier than males.

A pair of Cardinal Tetras, *Cheirodon axelrodi,* named in honor of the author by Dr. Leonard P. Schultz of the Smithsonian Institution. (*Photo by HRA.*)

Other Tetras

The popular name "Tetra" is given to many fish that look entirely unrelated. Tetras are usually classified according to their color. Platinum, silver, and blue are just a few of the prefixes that are added to the equally unorthodox name "Tetra."

From the Rio Taquary in Brazil comes *Hyphessobrycon herbertaxelrodi,* the Black Neon Tetra. There is a broad, velvety-black area on the lower half of the sides, topped by a glowing enamelwhite stripe above it. The upper half of the eye is bright red.

Spawning this beautiful fish can be accomplished in the same manner as described for Neons, and it falls into just about the same area as far as difficulty is concerned.

The Congo River in Africa gives us the gorgeous Congo Tetra, *Phenacogrammus interruptus.* With the sun shining on its opalescent scales, this fish is really a sight to behold, reflecting shades of blue, green, gold, and purple. A peculiarity of this species is in the middle rays of the tail fin, which become longer than the rest of the tail and resemble feathery appendages, especcially in the males.

The Black Neon, *Hyphessobrycon herbertaxelrodi,* has become an aquarium favorite. It makes an ideal community aquarium fish.

A pair of Congo Tetras, *Phenacogrammus interruptus.* Male below. The difference in sexes is clearly shown here by the male's flowing fins and the strange feathery elongation of the middle caudal rays. (*Photo by Milan Chvojka.*)

Silver Tetra (*Ctenobrycon spilurus*), from Guiana, a very graceful and flashy fish.

This species is rather large in size and takes a big tank for spawning. Eggs are laid among the plants near the bottom at a temperature of 75° to 77° F. and take six days to hatch. Of course the parents should be removed as soon as spawning is finished. The fry are quite large and able to take newly hatched brine shrimp at once.

The Black Tetra (*Gymnocorymbus ternetzi*), with its overly developed anal and dorsal fins, looks completely out of balance, with the majority of its mass being in the lower half of its body. The Tetra from Rio (*Hyphessobrycon flammeus*), with its beautiful red color, has a different type of anal and dorsal fin, but is similar to those of another type, the Yellow Tetra (*H. bifasciatus*), except that those of the latter are pale yellow. The Yellow Tetra looks much like the Dawn Tetra (*H. eos*).

The Glow Light Tetra (*H. gracilis*) appears to be more closely related to the Neon Tetra, just discussed, but breeds similarly to the Bettas in that it performs an embrace to facilitate fertilization of the eggs. It is a very colorful fish and easily bred.

Zebra Danio (*Brachydanio rerio*) is a very popular aquarium tropical.
Easily spawned, it races up and down the tank scattering eggs. This is an
interesting shot in that stroboscopic lights were used to slow down the action
of the fins. Though the picture was taken at less than 1/5000th of a
second, there is still action in the tails.

Zebra Fish
(Brachydanio rerio)

Among the most popular egg layers is the Zebra Fish (*Brachydanio rerio*), a good example of the misleading character of
popular names. Assuming that the Zebra Fish was named after
the familiar four-legged animal, we would expect to see a fish
with numerous vertical stripes, but such is not the case. The
Zebra Fish has three dark stripes running horizontally from the
head and through the tail along the body, not all like the striped
"horse." It belongs to the Cyprinidae, the Barb family.

The Zebra has long been a pet of the aquarium, especially
since it is so easily bred (with the help of a little imagination).
Its breeding habits do present a problem, however, as you will
see from the following description.

The Zebra breeds at high speeds, scattering eggs as it travels
the length of the aquarium and back in record time. The non-
adhesive eggs fall as they may, wherever they happen to be

dropped. In the average-size tank, at a water level of 8 inches, the Zebras can make two round trips before the light eggs hit the bottom of the tank. Should the parents pass a few falling eggs on their return, they will quickly eat them as they go, and then continue dropping, as though it were the most natural thing in the world. The aquarist must therefore find some system for the eggs to be trapped before the parents get a chance to catch them. Several methods have been devised, all being of equal value. One of the easiest to perform is a follows:

Place a long 20-gallon tank near a window; the sunlight will be beneficial for the propagation of algae and Infusoria. Fill the tank with no more than 4 inches of water. Put in no sand or plants. Purchase some large marbles, the larger the better (those about an inch in diameter are about the best). Sterilize the marbles by boiling them in water for twenty minutes. After the marbles have cooled—do not cool them by dropping them into cold water as this will crack them—cover the entire bottom of the tank with them to a depth of about 1 inch. Let the tank stay in the direct sunlight for a few hours each day for three days. Then select the female that looks most promising and place her in the tank just prepared. It is easy to recognize the female by her full, rounded body in comparison with the slimness of the male. Also, you can determine the sex, if you can spend time watching them, by the fact that the males chase the females. You will see that the male fish show amorous attention to the females when they are loaded and follow them very closely wherever they swim. If there is an empty female in the lot she will be noticed as a straggler. As soon as the female that you have placed in the new tank has become acquainted with her surroundings—it may take a day or two—place in with her three of four of the most active males, those that you have noticed have always been slim and fast. Do not choose a male straggler, as he will probably only eat the fertilized eggs instead of helping in their fertilization. The reason for selecting three or four males is twofold. First, in case there should

Glass Rasbora is nearly translucent.

Three-line Pencil Fish (*Nannostomus trifasciatus*).

An excellent pair of *Brachydanio frankei,* the Leopard Danio. The female, upper fish, is well filled with eggs. (*Photo by Milan Chvojka.*)

be any doubt, you want to be sure to have at least one male in the group; and second, assuming you are able to determine the sexes, it is best to have more than one male because if the female is well loaded she may drop more eggs than one male can fertilize.

After spawning, the female will be slimmer than she was before, and all the fish should be removed to their previous home. The eggs will hatch in fifty-six hours at 75° F. At first the young will grow faster and stronger if fed entirely on live food: Infusoria and then brine shrimp. After three weeks to a month, depending on their size, they may be fed fine dry food intermittently with the live food. Gordon's formula (p. 188) is also helpful, as are microworms, as they get larger.

Since Zebras get barely 2 inches long, and the young grow rather slowly (an inch in six months), it is best to keep them away from the larger fish, especially the Cichlids.

Newest of the *Brachydanio* species is *Brachydanio frankei,* the Leopard Danio, with a body that is speckled with tiny dots. They spawn just like the Zebra Danios, and are just as hardy. There is still doubt with many as to whether or not these are hybrids, but Meinken in Germany has classified them as a valid new species. Leopard Danios will cross with the other *Brachydanio* species and if the result is not sterile, there may come a time when it will not be easy to get a pure-bred pair.

All the Danios may be bred alike. It may be interesting to note that this is the same way in which Goldfish [2] spawn. See Appendix for further breakdown of the Danios.

[2] A friend of the author raises thousands of Goldfish yearly in several outdoor ponds. He spends quite a bit of money on marbles alone. Many of his goldfish are sold to lumber mills that introduce the fish into the lakes where lumber is stored, so they may devour certain types of aquatic insects that bore holes into the lumber. Goldfish ordinarily should never be introduced into natural waters, however, since they frequently become pests and cause harm to native fish. Moreover, they soon revert back to their ancestral dull, brassy coloration.

Sumatranus (*Capoeta tetrazona*), a popular Barb, is very active and colorful. Since they are high jumpers, a cover should be kept on their tank at all times.

Barbs

The Barbs are very desirable aquarium fish for manifold reasons: their gay, often loud coloring, their active movements, their formation when swimming, and the ease with which they may be spawned. Barbs are active eaters and not very choosy. They have occasionally been successfully reared on bread alone.

All the Barbs drop adhesive-type eggs and require live food in enormous quantities for successful breeding and maturation. They are at their best when exhibited in a large tank in great numbers, where they swim in active schools and soon learn to "beg for food." A person merely walking by the tank will cause a frantic race of the entire school to the spot where food is usually introduced. The feeding hole, usually left open in most aquarium covers, should be covered by a piece of glass at all times.

When you notice an individual fish getting very sluggish, remove it immediately and treat it with a solution of sodium bicarbonate. The Barbs have such phenomenal appetites that they usually overeat and may suffer as a result. It is a good habit to drop a teaspoon or two of bicarbonate of soda into the tank with the Barbs every other week. This procedure may be adapted for the community tank also.

Sumatranus
(*Capoeta tetrazona*)

As *Capoeta tetrazona,* often incorrectly called "Sumatranus" because it comes from Sumatra, is the most popular of the Barbs, we shall describe its peculiarities fully.[3]

If a person had heard the name "Zebra Fish" without knowing which fish bore that name, he would most likely assume it belonged to *C. tetrazona.* The *C. tetrazona* is striped like a Zebra, having four narrow bands of dark pigment running vertically completely around its body and head. It is gaily colored with yellow and red, though these colors tend to fade as the fish reaches maturity. Mr. Strasbourger has speciments that are over 2 inches in length and over 1 inch deep. He claims his success is owing to feeding the fish live food or fresh, peeled shrimp, morning and night, for the entire span of their life. (In feeding shrimp, care should be exercised that it does not cloud the water. Hang the shrimp in the tank on a thin silk thread and remove it after the fish seem to have had their fill.)

Since the *C. tetrazona* is a fast-swimming fish which drops sticky eggs when spawning, dense clumps of Nitella and similar plants must be provided to pick up the eggs.

Sex in these Barbs is easily distinguished. The female gets much

---

[3] The author wishes to thank Mr. Robert Strasbourger, of Brooklyn, New York, for giving freely of his valuable time in the preparation and coordination of the material on the Barbs. Mr. Strasbourger has been very successful in raising multitudes of the *Capoeta tetrazona.*

broader and rounder than the male, and while she loses much color, the male increases in color and develops a red "nose."

Seasoning for the female must take place in the breeding tank. Select the largest female and place her in the spawning tank. The spawning tank should be a long-type, 20-gallon size, at the minimum. Feed her large quantities of Tubifex and Daphnia with a medicine dropper, making sure that she is able to get all the food before it gets lost in the vegetation. A small area of the tank may be left bare for this feeding purpose. The males may be conditioned in the community tank by similar processes. Live food is essential for the seasoning of the fish. Dry food is dangerous for the *C. tetrazona* as they eat it too quickly and they tend to bloat when the food gets soaked.

When the female seems adjusted to her conditions and she looks as though she couldn't get much larger, place two males in with her. Spawning, just as in the Zebra Fish, should take place in a very short time.

While the fish are spawning, they should be fed Daphnia by the eyedropperful. If these small crustacea are not available, try Tubifex. With luck, the fish will take the food rather than the eggs; should they elect the eggs, do not continue the feeding of live food, but try to pull out the strands of Nitella that contain the eggs. Place these strands in a beaker filled with some of the same water in which the eggs were laid. Have the beaker floating in the spawning tank so it will be readily available for the deposit of the "egged down" Nitella and be at a constant temperature. Care should be exercised not to disturb the parents in the removal of the Nitella. *C. tetrazoma* is a great jumper and jumps at the slightest provocation. After the spawning, when the young fish have reached swimming size, every possible precaution should be taken to prevent them from jumping out. Mr. Strasbourger tells of fish jumping into the smallest cracks between the covering glass and the sides of the tank; how they manage to land on his living-room floor sometimes is a mystery even to him.

Black Tetra (*Gymnocorymbus ternetzi*), colorful and easily spawned.

The spawning just described should not take more than a few interesting hours, after which the parent fish should be removed and, if necessary, the eggs carefully replaced in the spawning tank. The spawn will hatch in two days, and must be fed Infusoria for the first few weeks. Follow this food with brine shrimp, microworms, or fine sifted Daphnia.

The optimum breeding temperature is 75° F. When the spawn are about three weeks old, raise the temperature to about 78° F. The lower spawning temperature helps slightly in keeping the bacterial count down.

In the other types of Barbs, the Rosy Barb (*Puntius conchonius*), Clown Barb (*Puntius everetti*), Black Ruby Barb (*Puntius nigrofasciatus*), Tic-tac-toe Barb (*Puntius ticto*), *et alia,* sex is easily determined by the size of the female, and breeding habits are the same as in the *Capoeta tetrazona.* Check the Appendix for specific breakdown.

Tic-tac-toe Barb (*Puntius ticto*), a silvery, scaly Barb.

White Cloud Mountain Fish (*Tanichthys albonubes*). These Chinese fish, from the White Cloud Mountain, are easily spawned when placed in a tank of their own with plenty of *Nitella*.

Giant Danio (*Danio malabaricus*), from the Malabar coast, is dangerous to small fish, though very peaceful with larger ones.

Hatchet Fish (*Gasteropelecus levis*). Fins are developed to help them skim above the surface of the water.

Geisha-girl Fish
(*Oryzias latipes*)

The many popular names attached to *Oryzias latipes,* such as "Geisha Girl," "Medaka," and "Rice Fish," give an indication of its popularity as an aquarium pet. Originally coming from Japan, where it was called "Medaka," the fish has many traits that tend to fix it as a permanent member of the exotic tropicals, holding the interest of many and varied fanciers.

Such a wealth of information is available on the Medaka that it would be possible to present the entire embryology. The value of such a complete study to the ordinary aquarist is doubtful, however, and, with a careful selection of the important material, a concise elementary study would seem to be more profitable.

The female Medaka possesses a single large ovary. This organ contains hundreds of eggs, all in different stages of development. As the eggs get more fully developed, they increase in size. This accounts for the swollen abdomen so characteristic of the female egg layer. The female may produce from one to eighty eggs a day, depending on various conditions. These eggs are squeezed out of the female's body by a special set of muscles in the tube called the "oviduct." They arrive outside the body of the female, hanging like a bunch of grapes, and are there fertilized by the male. One male may be active enough to service many females, thus it is to your advantage to have an abundance of females with a minimum number of males.

The eggs hang outside the body of the female for four or five hours, unless they happen to be brushed off by a plant or on the bottom of the tank. The Medaka will eat neither the eggs nor the young.

Care should be exercised in handling the Medakas as they are high jumpers. More peaceful aquarium fish are hard to find, and they further make themselves desirable by eating anything and everything, though they will make better parents if seasoned on live food.

Chapter 5
Scavengers

Catfish

The Catfish are easily identified by the whiskerlike barbels that extend from their "noses," "lips," and "chins." Another peculiarity is that the true Cats have no scales, though they sometimes possess a type of "shingle" which covers them. This "shingle" is very unlike the scales of ordinary fish, and, on some Catfish, looks much like the coats of armor worn by medieval knights; thus the name "Armored Catfish."

Most aquarists consider the Cats as merely scavengers. The Catfish are always busy poking their "snouts" into the gravel looking for any type of food. Dead leaves, food that has reached the bottom, dead snails, dead and decaying Daphnia are all of interest to Catfish, and they will devour them without much ado. The Cats are very peaceful, seldom attacking any live fish, regardless of size—there have been only a few substantiated reports about individual Cats eating small living fish. They will usually leave fish eggs alone, too, but when you spawn such fish as the Zebra Danio, which drop eggs onto the bottom of the tank, it would be more advisable to leave Cats out of the tank.

The author has observed Cats that were so bashful they would hide at the slightest provocation, yet when a school of Daphnia

Callichthys callichthys, a type of armored catfish, builds a bubble nest.

Electric Catfish actually gives off an electric charge and must be handled with insulated gloves. Its scientific name is *Malapterurus electricus.*

Armored Catfish such as *Corydoras paleatus* are good scavengers and are always poking about in the sand.

was introduced into the tank, they would make one of their rare appearances and swim out and help themselves. This, however, is a rare example, and not typical of the general behavior of Catfish.

Corydoras paleatus

Though the Cats are very seldom bred by the amateur, they will breed rather easily, and very interestingly. Let us consider *Corydoras paleatus* as the typical Catfish for the home aquarium. The *Corydoras* are the small members of the family Callichthyidae, and are very well suited for the small tank.

The *C. paleatus* is among the most popular of tropical fish, not because of beauty, but for its great assistance to the keeper of an aquarium in his cleaning. *C. paleatus* also breeds to a large extent like many of the more beautiful fish kept in tanks for aesthetic reasons.

A pair of *Corydoras paleatus*. (*Photo by Dr. Herbert R. Axelrod.*)

Since sex in the Cats is very difficult to distinguish, breeding must be accomplished by natural pairing. Some authors think that a comparison of the ventral fins will offer a sexual distinction. This method is difficult to use, not only because the fins are so similar in shape, but also because the Cats are nearly always in a position that makes comparison of the ventral fins impossible. These ventral fins are important in the reproductive cycle of the fish.

Should you have half a dozen mature Cats in the same tank, you might notice a male staying very close to a female, showing her more than a usual amount of attention. After a few hours of close movement on the bottom of the tank, the female will assume a position across the male that will facilitate her catching his flowing milt in her mouth. This milt is colorless and invisible; the author has attempted on various occasions to introduce some sort of dye into the male that might color his sperm but has had no success.

THIS PAGE: *Corydoras axelrodi,* from the Rio Meta in Colombia. (*Photo by Dr. Herbert R. Axelrod.*)

The Pygmy Corydoras, *Corydoras hastatus,* attains a top size of only 1½ inches. (*Photo by G. J. M. Timmerman.*)

FACING PAGE: *Corydoras melanistius* looks as if it were wearing a mask. (*Photo by Milan Chvojka.*)

Corydoras arcuatus is called the Skunk Catfish because of the line that runs along its back. (*Photo by G. J. M. Timmerman.*)

It seems that as soon as the female has the milt in her mouth, she drops a few eggs, catching them between her ventral fins. She then leaves the prostrate male and searches for a suitable location for her eggs. When a stiff leaf has been selected, she touches the spot with her mouth, there depositing some milt, and then presses a couple of eggs into the milt. She repeats this process very shortly to dispose of the remaining eggs she has clasped in between her ventral fins. The female will then return to the male.

The female does not usually drop all her eggs in one place; she more often seeks a new place for each quartet of eggs. Different types of Cats are interested in different types of locations, some choosing the glass, some even a bubble nest.

The eggs hatch in a few days, and the young immediately disappear into the muck on the bottom of the tank, where they seem to stay for a few weeks until they are large enough to handle fairly large-sized food (grown Daphnia). They mature rapidly and seem very hardy. The parents show little interest in their brood and, if well fed, usually will not disturb the eggs. Other Cats will not bother the brood either.

Among the other types of Cats that are popular are the *C. aeneus,* a type that breeds by the female placing her eggs on glass; the Leopard Cat (*C. julii*), a very active fish; *C. nattereri,* which is very similar in all respects to the *C. paleatus,* though slightly darker; and the large, 4-inch *C. agassizi.*

All these Cats are peaceful, very hardy, and excellent as scavengers. They will do especially well if kept on a diet of live food (Tubifex is best; Cats can often dig it out of the sand by burrowing, while it is usually too deep to be pulled out by the more ordinary types of aquarium fish) and in a tank of their own. Best breeding results will be obtained if a blanket of algae is allowed to accumulate on the bottom of the tank so the fish may hide when they feel shy. This cover will also be beneficial to the young *Corydoras.*

Corydoras julii is a very attractive and popular species. (*Photo by G. J. M. Timmerman.*)

Corydoras aeneus, the Bronze Catfish, is one of the hardiest and most available Catfishes. (*Photo by Milan Chvojka.*)

Otocinclus affinis from Brazil is a fair scavenger.

Glass Catfish (*Kryptopterus bicirrhis*). The entire skeletal structure of this
fish is visible.

Glass Catfish
(*Kryptopterus bicirrhis*)

This fish, though not a real scavenger, earns a place in this material as a member of the Catfish family.

As the name "Glass" implies, this species of Catfish is very nearly transparent. It may reach 3 inches in length and is rather shy and timid. It is not a bottom feeder, but catches food on the way down. It usually does not feed from the top either.

Though rather harmless, it does go after young fish.

Breeding is apparently very difficult, and sex in the Glass Cat is hard to determine.

Other Scavangers

Certain fish are peculiarly adapted to do the work of a scavenger. The habit of the *Corydoras,* namely their preference for feeding off the bottom, makes them ideal for this purpose. But other fish have the same property which also should make them desirable for cleaning purposes. The common Guppy picks continually on any palatable matter that may be on the bottom of the tank, and is often used for scavenging purposes. The name "scavenger," when used in connection with a certain class of fish, is much like the term "weed" when talking about a garden. Is a stray orchid a weed in a patch of dandelions? Yes, if you are primarily interested in raising dandelions! But there is bound to be trouble if the general name "scavenger" is used too freely.

The many fish that have tremendous appetites all might well be called "scavengers," but there must be a distinction: A scavenger is a fish that eats food which is left uneaten by the other fish in the tank. (Such animals as snails, clams, mussels, and shrimp may be included in this category.)

Scavengers eat not only food which the others have left behind,

Gyrinocheilus aymonieri, the "Chinese" Algae Eater, actually comes from Thailand. (*Photo by Wilhelm Hoppe.*)

but there are those which get into places where the other ones cannot squeeze and pick up whatever is left there. Such a group are the ones known as the Kuhli Loaches, which includes *Acanthophthalmus kuhli, A. semicinctus, A. shelfordi,* and *A. myersi.* These Loaches have about the same body shape, elongated and snakelike, which lets them crowd into some very tight corners and get bits of food which would otherwise contribute toward fouling the tank.

Another type of "scavenger" has come to be known extensively as the Chinese Algae Eater, *Gyrinocheilus aymonieri.* Whoever gave them the "Chinese" part of their name must have had an active imagination, because they come from Thailand, quite a stretch away from China. These fish have a very greedy appetite for algae, and spend a great deal of their time foraging for it. They go over the glass sides of the tank, the rocks, plants, and gravel, and keep plucking at all the algal growths that come their way.

A sucker-mouth Catfish using its mouth to clean the aquarium glass.
(*Photo by G. J. M. Timmerman.*)

An immature *Xenocara dolichoptera*. When maturity approaches, the small
spots disappear and the "whiskers" become longer and bushy. (*Photo by
(Harald Schultz.*)

G. aymonieri is not alone in being a fish that will eat great amounts of algae. There are *Plecostomus, Otocinclus, Hyposto-mus,* and *Xenocara* species, all from tropical South America, which graze happily on algal growths and bits of uneaten food. As far as looks go, they are just about the unloveliest fishes in existence. With many of them this is the secret of their charm. They rarely spawn in captivity.

At one time it was believed to be necessary for every well-set-up aquarium to have a few snails, but this is not so. Snails have their "pros" and "cons," which we list here:

1. A snail consumes oxygen as well as a fish. For every snail you must figure one less fish of similar dimensions.

2. Snails greedily consume great amounts of algae, it is true. They often raise havoc with your valued plants as well.

3. A snail will dutifully clean up uneaten food but will also leave behind it a number of messy droppings.

4. Snails are very prolific, and disposing of the young often becomes a problem.

So there you have it. They have their good points, but in order to benefit by their good points, you have to put up with their faults.

It is well known that Daphnia feed readily on most types of Infusoria and green algae, and it is standard practice to introduce Daphnia into a tank that is cloudy or green. In doing this, one caution, however: *Remove the fish.* Not only could the fish over-eat and thus reduce the number of scavengers, but the tank might not be able to support so much life at one time. The water could become too saturated with carbon dioxide and thus poison all the inhabitants, or the fish might turn on one another and kill themselves, which often happens in densely populated aquaria.

Sometimes fresh-water clams or mussels are placed in the tank to help keep the water clear. These animals serve their purpose well as they obtain food by sucking water through a set of filters

This tank contains different types of shelled scavengers. Mussels and various types of snails are good scavengers. (*Courtesy General Biological Supply House.*)

and thus remove most types of suspensions, whether digestible or not. Although these animals have unusual capacities for clearing water, they do represent a hazard. Should one die, it might go unnoticed for a few days, since they are not very visibly active, and their decaying would do more damage than they could ever do good. Also, several large fish may peck at them, causing them untold grief; or, as the author has witnessed, large fish (*Astronotus ocellatus*) may try to ingest them—*Bettas* also make their lives miserable.

Snails are undoubtedly the favorite as far as shelled scavengers go. They reproduce without any help, often producing a type of very nutritious egg that is enjoyed by many fish. Some snails produce live young (Japanese Live Bearer). It might be worth while to discuss individually each of the popular types of snails and their advantages, since they are so valuable when put to the proper task.

Japanese Live-bearing Snail

Most fresh-water snails are hermaphroditic, that is to say, each individual snail has both male and female reproductive organs, and they can also fertilize their own eggs. This sexual independence does not stop two snails from acting as male and female together, as well. The few exceptions to the rule are the dioecious (either male or female) type which belong to the genus *Viviparus*. The Japanese Snail is that type of snail in which reproduction requires the participation of a male and female of the species. This does not mean that if you have kept a female Japanese Snail alone for several months she cannot have a brood. Quite to the contrary. The Japanese Snail is purported to have only one fertilization a lifetime. This fertilization must take care of the entire mass of unfertilized eggs which are contained in the body of the female. The eggs are hatched in a space under the shell of the female, where they remain until they emerge as fully recognizable snails.

Red Ramshorn
(*Planorbis corneus*)

The Red Ramshorn (*Planorbis corneus*) Snail is one of the larger types of snails available for the home aquarium. When placed in a tank with Daphnia, they reproduce magnificently. These snails must be fed a type of food which tends to produce profuse cultures of Infusoria; lettuce, celery greens, spinach, and oatmeal mush are excellent. Daphnia must be used to clear the tank of too much Infusoria, since an overabundance of these small creatures is detrimental to the health of the snails.

LEFT: Red Ramshorn (*Planorbis corneus*), an algae eater and good food for Cichlids.

RIGHT: Mystery Snail (*Ampullaria cuprina*).

Given the proper care and aeration, and at a temperature of about 78° F., the Red Ramshorn will reproduce rapidly. Eggs are laid in groups of from eight to thirty and hatch out in about three weeks. Care should be exercised in choosing the type of fish to be introduced into the tank with the Red Ramshorn. Cichlids will eat them when they are small, and all fish will readily take their undeveloped eggs. Many aquarists place the Reds in their aquaria in order to provide some extra living food for their fish.

Mystery Snail
(*Ampullaria cuprina*)

The Mystery Snail (Apple Snail) gets its name from its peculiar breeding habits. The fact that it needs a dry area upon which to spawn, coupled with the fact that the developing embryos need dry spaces to develop, makes breeding very difficult in the ordinary aquarium.

The Mystery Snails are not dioecious and are extremely valuable in tanks where Infusoria is required in quantity. In the process of digesting the greens that should be provided for the Infusoria as well as the snails, the Mystery Snail excretes organic matter that serves as excellent food to the Infusoria protozoa. These snails should not be placed in a spawning tank until the young have hatched, as they eat fish eggs.

Unless they are provided with a substantial diet of greens, the Mysteries may attack growing plants, so it is wise always to keep a piece of lettuce in the tank.

Pond Snails
(*Lymnaea, Physa*)

The two familiar forms of Pond Snails seem to differ only in the type of twist they possess. The *Lymnaea* curls to the left, the *Physa* to the right.

The Pond Snails are not dioecious and reproduce by cementing sticky masses of eggs on the plants and glass parts of the aquarium. These eggs are too hard to be eaten by most fish, though Cichlids and Bettas seem to enjoy them. As they usually reproduce in geometric progression, they are the most prolific snails in the average home tank. A mass of eggs will have hatched in three weeks, and in another three months these, in turn, will have eggs of their own.

Other types of snails will usually serve the same general purpose but are not so plentiful as the aforementioned.

Care should be exercised to remove all dead snails. They might cloud the water should they be allowed to decompose in the tank. If snails become too plentiful, they may be crushed between the fingers so the fish may clean the meat from the shells. The empty shells may supply a few necessary minerals to the plants.

Chapter 6
The "Annual" Fishes

Mother Nature, as all who study her ways can attest, has many strange ways of keeping the world populated with her creatures. In many places in the tropical areas of Africa and South America there are spots where bodies of water fill to overflowing during the rainy season, but when the dry season comes along these places dry out completely. How can a fish live in these holes? And if he can, what happens when there is no more water? Let us examine the very strange life cycle of this beautiful group of Killifishes.

The rainy season comes on with a series of downpours on the parched land, and in the ponds and ditches that were dried out all during the hot, dry season water gradually appears and becomes deeper. Tiny fishes appear as if by magic, and the water soon teems with them. They grow at an unbelievable rate, and in a few months become sexually mature and mate, burying their eggs in the bottom silt. The males find territories for themselves and battle fiercely for them when another male appears, showing their most brilliant colors.

But this happy state of affairs does not last very long. The rains soon end, and the hot sun makes itself felt on the water. The result, of course, is much less water, and the fish become more and more crowded. Predators appear on the scene, as they always do when there is an easy meal at hand: kingfishers, cranes, egrets, and many others. As time goes on only the deeper spots, or what

A pair of *Nothobranchius rachovi*. Male above. (*Photo by E. Roloff.*)
A male *Nothobranchius guentheri*. (*Photo by Milan Chvojka.*)

A pair of *Cynolebias nigripinnis*. Male below. The male's colors have been compared to stars in a midnight sky. (*Photo by Günter Senfft.*)

Pterolebias peruensis comes from the tributaries of the upper Amazon. The male is below. (*Photo by M. F. Roberts.*)

were the deeper spots, still hold water, and soon these dry out as well. The fish? They die by the millions when there is not enough water to support them and what were lovely, lush ponds become foul, malodorous spots.

Mercifully, decay is rapid in the tropics and these areas soon become dried-out holes which bear little resemblance to what they once were. No water, but the fish life is there just the same, in the form of eggs left by the breeding fish during the rainy season. They buried their eggs in the bottom silt, you will recall. These eggs, protected from the direct rays of the sun by this covering of silt, undergo a partial drying at this time.

Then the inevitable change of seasons takes place once more and the rain again begins falling. Life awakens within these eggs, which hatch in short order and start their strange, short life cycle all over again.

In Africa, these "annual" fishes are represented by the *Nothobranchius* species in the Mozambique area in the east, and some of the *Aphyosemion* species in the west. This genus has two entirely different ways of spawning. Most species simply hang their eggs on plant leaves, where they hatch in two weeks, but the ones we treat here are the bottom-spawning species, *Aphyosemion sjoestedti, A. coeruleum,* and *A. arnoldi.* These two genera include some of the loveliest of all aquarium fishes and are very high in cost, taking into consideration the short life span, which rarely exceeds eight months. In South America there are the *Cynolebias* and *Pterolebias* species, which have exactly similar life spans.

To the fish breeder, propagating these species presents the problem of giving them similar conditions in the aquarium. Most of these species when mature and well conditioned are ready to spawn any time a male can swim up to a female. So eager are the males to spawn that many breeders make it a point to use two or three females to every male. A 10-gallon aquarium is ample in most cases. The bottom is covered with peat moss which has been well boiled in advance. Here they find a substitute for the soft mud of their habitat and lose little time digging in close beside each other and depositing eggs. Water temperature should be about 78° F., and the tank should be kept covered to keep the fish from jumping out. Live Daphnia and Tubifex worms are the desirable foods for conditioning, with an occasional feeding of white worms. Once the female has become depleted of eggs, which is shown by her lessened girth, she and the male should be taken out and kept separate until they recuperate in a week or so. This leaves a tank with a good supply of eggs buried in the peat moss. The water is then emptied carefully until there is only the wet peat moss left, and at this time the drying process is duplicated by allowing the peat moss to become partially dry and then covering the tank.

At this time a little patience is called for: the eggs must remain as they are for six weeks. Then a few inches of water is poured back into the tank. In a short time, sometimes a very short time, the fry will be seen swimming about. Sometimes the eggs are not yet fully developed, in which case they will not hatch. Leaving them dried out for another week may do the trick, and the process may have to be repeated a few times; sometimes a few hatch before the others.

Granted the eggs have hatched, you will note that the yolk sacs have been absorbed and they swim freely. They are large enough at this time to eat newly hatched brine shrimp and feedings should be frequent, as they consume unbelievable amounts. Growth is very rapid, as may be expected when their original home conditions are considered.

All this seems to be a lot of trouble to go to for a fish that will live for only about eight months, but this group of Killifishes is among the most beautiful of all aquarium fishes. You may not have them for a long time, but they are certainly a thing of beauty while they last!

Chapter 7
Plants

Let any person who believes that the only important part of an aquarium is the fish keep his fish in a bare tank, and he will soon realize the value of plants.

A critical review of what plants do for the home aquarium—as well as what they do not do—has been made Dr. James W. Atz. The following section is composed of his article on this controversial subject.[1]

Although plants have been grown in home aquaria for more than a hundred years, their functions in such small bodies of water are still largely misunderstood. Not only aquarists, but teachers and scientists as well, have entertained incorrect ideas about the part that plants play in the so-called "balanced aquarium" ever since vegetation was first put into the tanks with fish. Strangely enough, this century of error has not handicapped the keepers of home aquaria to any great extent. Being empirically minded, aquarists have accepted and employed practices and techniques that "worked," without concerning themselves too much as to just *why* they worked. This practical attitude has produced beautiful tanks and healthy fish but has sometimes placed

---

[1] Atz, J. W., "The Functions of Plants in Aquaria," *Aquarium Journal,* 21: 40, 56, 1950.

fish fanciers in the comfortable but somewhat strange position of doing the right thing for the wrong reason.

There are perhaps half a dozen different reasons why the aquarist should try to keep plants in his aquarium, but the oxygenation of tank water is *not* one of them. In fact, the idea that the fish and plants of an aquarium balance each other in their production and consumption of carbon dioxide and oxygen is a false one—of such long standing and general acceptance that it perhaps deserves to be called a myth.

The usual concept of the balanced aquarium is quite simple—a little too pat, it turns out. Fish and aquatic plants utilize the gases, oxygen and carbon dioxide, that are *dissolved* in water. Animals, including fish, of course, respire, taking in oxygen and giving off carbon dioxide. Plants also respire, but in the presence of light that is strong enough and of the proper wave lengths they also carry on the process of photosynthesis as a result of which carbon dioxide and water are taken in and oxygen released. In the actively photosynthesizing plant, this process well overbalances that of respiration so that the *net* result is the consumption of carbon dioxide and production of oxygen.

The respiring animal "burns" carbohydrates and other energy-producing materials and obtains energy. On the other hand, the photosynthesizing plant stores up energy in manufactured food with the aid of green chlorophyll. Here is a chemical simplification of the essential processes involved:

$$6H_2O + 6CO_2 \underset{\text{photosynthesis}}{\overset{\text{respiration}}{\rightleftharpoons}} C_6H_{12}O_6 + 6O_2$$

water   carbon   glucose   oxygen
        dioxide

It is obvious that these processes counterbalance one another, and it might be thought that this is evidence in favor of the idea that plants balance fish in an aquarium. This reasoning involves one false assumption, however; namely that an aquarium is a closed

Not too many plants are necessary in home aquaria. The plants in a tank
do not increase the number of fish the tank will support.

system, cut off completely from the outside world. To be more
specific, the oxygen and carbon dioxide in the air above the water
have not been taken into consideration.

It was Dr. Charles M. Breder, Jr., who first pointed out that
the oxygen dissolved in the water of an aquarium comes, not from
the plants, but from the atmosphere. He found that whenever
tank water was oversaturated or undersaturated with oxygen to
the slightest degree, it very quickly returned to equilibrium with
the oxygen in the air above—whether or not plants were present
or whether the measurements were taken in bright sunlight or in
the dark. Obviously plants could not have been affecting the

oxygen content of the water to any significant extent. The oxygen comes in from the air as fast as the smallest deficiency exists in the water. Similarly, surplus oxygen immediately passes off into the atmosphere whenever any excess is present. Except under extraordinary conditions, there is neither any lack nor excess of oxygen in an aquarium.

How is it, then, that fish sometimes seem to "smother" so obviously—in an overcrowded aquarium, for example? The answer is that carbon dioxide causes their distress and eventually kills them. According to experiments made by physiologists, fish can be killed by carbon dioxide even though there is plenty of oxygen present. Carbon dioxide moves in and out of water much more slowly than oxygen. When aquatic plants were actively engaged in photosynthesis, Breder found that the amount of carbon dioxide in tank water remained far below the equilibrium point. In other words, plants can use up carbon dioxide more rapidly than the carbon dioxide can enter the water from the air. Similarly, dissolved carbon dioxide can accumulate in an aquarium more rapidly than it is able to pass off into the atmosphere. Unless the carbon dioxide content is then reduced in some way, the fish are unable to adjust themselves to the excessive accumulation of this gas and may die—even though there is plenty of oxygen all around them. It should be realized that the amount of carbon dioxide dissolved in water is to all intents and purposes independent of the amount of dissolved oxygen, and vice versa.

When fish come gaping to the top of an aquarium, the cause is an excess of carbon dioxide, not a deficiency of oxygen—except under extraordinary conditions when an oxygen deficiency may exist. For instance, a tank that has gone completely "bad" may contain so many bacteria that the oxygen content of its water is kept dangerously low. Even in such an aquarium, however, the accumulation of carbon dioxide must also play a part in causing the distress of fish, since bacteria produce this gas just as do higher plants and animals.

It has been shown *in experimental tanks* that the greater the carbon dioxide content of water, the higher must be the concentration of oxygen to "offset" its harmful effects. Anything that tends both to lower the oxygen and increase the carbon dioxide will have a doubly detrimental effect, so to speak.[2] Nevertheless, Breder's measurements show that carbon dioxide, not oxygen, is the limiting gas, so far as respiration is concerned, under all ordinary conditions in aquaria.

Carbon dioxide and not oxygen should therefore be the aquarist's concern. When a tank is aerated artificially by air pumps, very little, if any, oxygen is being introduced—since the water is practically saturated with that gas at all times—but the release of carbon dioxide is being facilitated—carbon dioxide which can build up to dangerously high concentrations, since it can be produced more rapidly than it can escape into the atmosphere. In effect, the myriads of tiny bubbles rising from an aerator increase the surface through which the gas can leave the water. As has been emphasized by a number of experienced fish fanciers, the surface of water exposed to the atmosphere is the all-important factor in a standing aquarium. In calculating the number of fish that a certain tank will comfortably support, the most critical element is the area of the water's surface, not the volume. Another result of aeration may be the circulation of water within the tank, preventing stratification and bringing carbon-dioxide-laden water to the surface.

It is often said that keeping plants in an aquarium will enable it to maintain more fish. If plants were actively photosynthesizing

[2] High temperature is such a factor, since it decreases the amount of oxygen (and carbon dioxide) that water can hold in solution, but increases the rate at which carbon dioxide is produced by speeding up the metabolism of the fish. It is true that less carbon dioxide can be held in solution, but this gas, we must remember, often builds up concentrations above its saturation point, a thing that oxygen does not do. Rising temperatures therefore cause a relative increase in the carbon dioxide content of aquarium water, if not an absolute one.

at all times, they would keep down the carbon-dioxide concentration appreciably, as Breder showed, thus permitting more fish to live in a given tank. But plants continually respire, just as animals do, and it is only in bright light that their respiration is more than offset by photosynthesis with the net result that carbon dioxide is consumed and oxygen produced. At night or on dark days, they are not engaged in photosynthesis and produce carbon dioxide and consume oxygen exactly as fish do. At such times, the presence of plants theoretically lessens the number of fish a tank will support. The amounts of gas exchanged by plants during respiration are much less than those by animals, however, so it is doubtful whether the consumption of oxygen and production of carbon dioxide by plants are ever of sufficient magnitude to cause aquarium fish any trouble. For this reason, the aquarist need hardly ever worry about having his tank too heavily planted. In all probability, a tank would have to be almost completely choked with plants before any effect would become noticeable.

Anyone who wants proof that plants are not essential to any so-called "balanced aquarium" need only remove all of them from such a tank; the fish will show no respiratory distress whatsoever. This simple experiment should convince aquarists that plants do not oxygenate the water in an aquarium. They should not wonder, however, at their long-standing misapprehension in these matters, because only one leader in the field has ever tried to set them right—Christopher W. Coates, Director Emeritus of the New York Aquarium.

Since plants act as oxygenators only to an insignificant extent in an aquarium, it might be thought that they are useless or even deleterious. That such a view is completely erroneous will be apparent from the following remarks, outlining the principal functions of plants in aquaria. For convenience, these have been treated under six different headings:

1. *To decorate the tank.* This is put first even though it may seem the least utilitarian. If aquaria could not be made attractive

or an asset to the appearance of a room, how many fish fanciers would there be? To be sure, there are many who are interested in fish *per se,* but by and large it is the beauty of a well-decorated tank that attracts people to the hobby. We believe that the vegetation of an aquarium is by far the greatest contributor to its beauty.

2. *To minimize the likelihood of excessive multiplication of algae.* In general, tanks that are well planted suffer less frequently from green water or any other overabundance of algae. This phenomenon has also been noticed in outdoor ponds and pools and has been demonstrated experimentally out-of-doors. Several theories have been advanced to explain why it occurs. One is that the large plants shade the water sufficiently to prevent the growth of the small types, but it seems unlikely that this could happen in a glass-sided tank. Another idea is that the large plants produce some substance inhibiting the growth of the small ones, but no one has yet detected such a material.

A third theory has been suggested by Dr. C. M. Breder, Jr., and other workers. Since plant physiologists have shown that plants are dependent upon a number of substances for growth, a well-established stand of higher plants may use up one or more of the available growth-promoting materials as fast as they appear in an aquarium, or keep them at so low a level that no large amount of algae can be formed. Johnstone's application of Liebig's Law of the Minimum to planktonic growth is perhaps pertinent here: "A plant requires a certain number of foodstuffs if it is to continue and grow, and each of these food substances must be present in a certain proportion. If one of them is absent, the plant will die; if one is present in a minimal proportion, the growth will also be minimal. This will be the case no matter how abundant the other foodstuffs may be. Thus the growth of a plant is dependent upon the amount of that foodstuff which is presented to it in minimal quantity." Drs. F. W. Kavanagh and H. W. Rickett of the New York Botanical Garden have pointed out,

The effect of top lighting is easily seen in the shadows and soft appearance of the aquarium. The plants are growing toward the light.

however, that the amounts of nitrogenous and mineral substances used by plants in an ordinary aquarium are minute and unlikely to become a limiting factor. In fact, ordinary tap water is often a pretty good nutrient solution for plants, the very small amount of materials dissolved in it being sufficient for them. The reason a good growth of higher plants tends to prevent excessive multiplication of algae is thus a mystery, and if the Law of the Minimum applies, it does not concern the fertilizing substances in fish wastes since these are present far in excess of the plants' needs.

Many aquarists have believed that plants help maintain a more nearly uniform water chemistry in an aquarium by utilizing appreciable quantities of the nitrogenous wastes of fish. Because the amounts of these fertilizers necessary for aquatics' growth are

This is a beautiful, natural setting. Note the short Amazon Sword Plant in the center.

insignificant compared to what the fish are producing, this effect does not operate to any extent. In this connection, it should be remembered that fish have been known to live in unplanted tanks for years without any change of water. They have also lived for long periods in standing aquaria kept in total darkness, where not even algae can grow.

3. *To provide food for the fish, both directly and indirectly, by promoting the growth of various micro-organisms and other small animals.* Fish that eat leafy plants are not popular with the great majority of aquarists, so the use of higher plants directly as fish food is relatively unimportant. Only algae are regularly eaten by the common species of tropical fish kept in aquaria. Indirectly, however, leafy plants and stoneworts may be quite

important. The behavior of many fish gives ample demonstration of this, for they spend much time picking or grazing on the leaves and stems of submerged aquatics. In nature a great variety of very small creatures lives on aquatic plants. Undoubtedly fewer exist on the plants in aquaria, but, so far as we know, they help provide a more adequate and natural diet for captive fish. Nitella, one of the stoneworts or Charales, is especially valuable in this regard.

4. *To shelter less dominant fish from attacks of their more aggressive neighbors.* A careful study of the behavior of practically any group of fish in captivity reveals that certain individuals dominate others whenever there is competition for food, swimming space, or potential mates. Sometimes this domination appears to border on persecution, and the only way a less aggressive fish may be able to escape harassment from its more domineering tankmate is by hiding. Nothing can provide more or better hiding places in an aquarium than a generous growth of plants. It has also been demonstrated that dividing a tank into partially separated compartments reduces the amount of aggressive behavior among territory-holding fish, apparently by enabling them to establish their domains securely with less fighting. It would seem quite probable that plants act in a similar way, providing fish with niches, nooks, or crannies that they can call their own, so to speak, or as refuges when hard pressed by some other fish.

5. *To provide sites for the attachment of eggs and refuges for the protection of young fish.* These are well-recognized functions of aquatic plants. A large number of different fish place or scatter their eggs on plants. Among the better known genera that include species with such reproductive habits are: *Hyphessobrycon, Hemigrammus, Nannostomus, Poecilobrycon, Barbodes, Puntius, Capoeta, Carassius, Rasbora, Corydoras, Rivulus, Epiplatys, Nematocentrus, Pachypanchax, Aplocheilus, Pterophyllum,* and *Chanda.* For baby fish, hiding places are life-or-death matters. Without a suitable sanctuary from hungry larger fish, few young

Healthy fish in a healthy tank.

would survive. A heavy growth of floating plants seems to be the best protection for tiny fish, and it also provides them with good feeding grounds for microscopic and near-microscopic prey.

6. *To give the fish a natural habitat, more conducive to their well-being—in the broadest sense of the term.* This somewhat intangible function of plants is placed last because it forms a sort of catch-all for any items not included in the first five—most of which it overlaps in several respects. It is quite reasonable to suppose that, in general, captive fish will behave more normally, be more healthy, and will live longer and more natural lives, the more closely their man-made environment approximates or betters their native environment. Plants form an integral part of the natural habitat of most tropical fish; for this reason, if no other, the aquarist should give them careful consideration.

Undoubtedly some of the functions of plants in aquaria have been omitted from the above. For example, Dr. Myron Gordon has found that Nitella can be used to condition raw tap water. It is nevertheless evident that fish benefit greatly from the presence of plants in their aquaria.

The benefits that accrue from keeping plants and fish together do not extend only to the fish, however; the plants, too, profit from the association. It is common experience that aquatic plants grow better when kept with fish than when kept alone, provided, of course, that the fish are not of the plant-molesting type. Aquatic plants need fertilizer just as terrestrial ones do, and fish wastes are evidently excellent fertilizer, although fish produce far in excess of what the plants require. Of much greater importance is the carbon dioxide given off by the fish. There is good evidence that this gas is usually a limiting factor in the growth of at least the higher aquatic plants. Without it photosynthesis cannot take place, and these plants apparently quickly exhaust the supply dissolved in water. Breder's measurements of carbon dioxide concentrations in aquaria lend support to this view, since he found that the carbon dioxide remained far below its equilibrium point with the atmosphere for long periods when the plants in an aquarium were actively photosynthesizing. A more adequate supply of carbon dioxide is undoubtedly the reason plants kept with fish grow better than those kept in old tanks rich in fish wastes but without any fish.

For both utilitarian and aesthetic reasons, aquatic plants should be an essential part of the home aquarium, and successful aquarists will continue to use them generously.

In selecting aquatic plants, careful consideration should be given each individual species and its physical requirements. Following are discussions of the most important of these plants.

Anacharis
(*Elodea canadensis*)

An important plant in practically any type of aquarium is the popular Anacharis, more commonly called "Elodea." This plant may be purchased at any store that carries fish of any kind. As noted in the discussion of the balanced aquarium, the amount of oxygen that a plant gives off during its growth (photosynthesis) is of little importance to the amount of oxygen dissolved in the water; oxygen that is needed would more readily be picked up from the air that is in contact with the water surface. Many dealers, as well as authors of texts on tropical fish, might nevertheless be tempted to claim that Anacharis is the best plant for oxygenating purposes. As explained above, this is not so. Plants should be selected for other purposes. If you are looking for a plant that will reproduce quickly and beautifully in a tank that gets a few hours of direct sunlight a day, as well as a plant that will offer considerable protection to fish and young during spawning time, Anacharis is the answer. The only drawback to including Anacharis in every type of tank is that it needs a certain minimum amount of direct sunlight, or equivalent artificial light, per day to maintain its fineness. This is true of most of the cheaper and more popular plants. Should you attempt to raise the Anacharis in a dark tank, it would become stringy and scrawny, developing more and more space between its leaves.

When Anacharis is purchased from a dealer, it usually comes in bunches bound together at the bottom with a strip of lead. Remove the lead and tear off about an inch of the bottom of the plant. Then stick the stems into about an inch of sand. The arrangement of the plants is important mostly for aesthetic reasons. It is usually wiser to have the taller growing plants in the rear and sides of the aquarium so the smaller ones may be easily seen. Should taller plants be placed all through the tank, the fish will not be shown off to their best advantage since they will always be partially hidden by the vegetation.

Milfoil
(*Myriophyllum spicatum*)

The long, fine leaves of this plant afford maximum efficiency in catching the eggs of the egg-laying fish. It needs plenty of strong light to maintain its closely knit leaves. When such light is

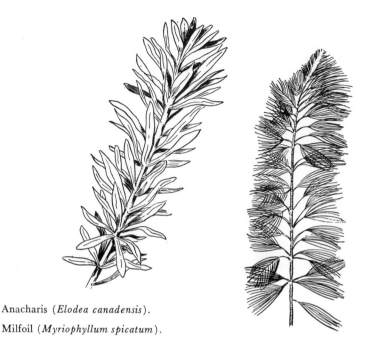

Anacharis (*Elodea canadensis*).
Milfoil (*Myriophyllum spicatum*).

afforded the plant, it will grow astoundingly fast, sometimes as much as 3 or 4 inches a week. This plant is very sensitive to the salt-permanganate solution and should be removed from any tank undergoing such a treatment.

Plant Myriophyllum the same way as Anacharis, tearing off an inch or so before putting it in the sand. Should growth be too rapid, the plant may be uprooted and left to float around in the water. In time, however, it will send down fine roots into the sand. All plants seem to be able to distinguish between the top of the aquarium and the bottom. This property is known as "geotropism." If plants bend toward the source of light, "phototropism"—and they all should—make sure that the light is placed directly above them. Should one lamp suffice for the entire tank, all the plants will grow toward that light.

Fanwort (*Cabomba caroliniana*).

Tape Grass (*Vallisneria americana*).

Fanwort
(Cabomba caroliniana)

This plant looks like a cross between the Anacharis and the Myriophyllum; it has properties common to each and acts like both of them. More than the rest, it requires a great amount of light to maintain its dense appearance. Should there be insufficient light, it will tend to become very stringy.

The author uses Cabomba in a demonstration tank at New York University. This tank contains a few hundred Guppies and, other than a little green algae, Cabomba is its sole plant. It gets exactly eight hours of light from three 25-watt bulbs a day, six days a week. The Cabomba does so well that specimens 3 or 4 feet long have been taken from it. Recently, one of the plants flowered, giving off eight blossoms. The blossoms were miniature lilies, a really beautiful sight.

Cabomba should be treated the same as Anacharis.

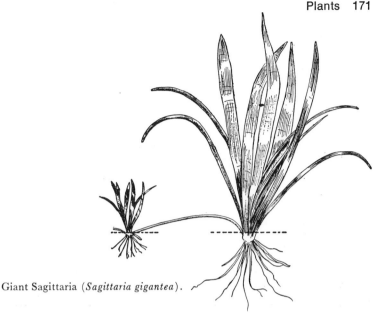

Giant Sagittaria (*Sagittaria gigantea*).

Tape Grass
(*Vallisneria americana*)

Vallisneria americana, though not the most familiar type to be used in the home aquarium, is of tremendous importance for all sorts of wild life; muskrats, fish, ducks, and geese all relish this plant and eat it readily.

The Vallisneria reproduces by sending out runners, which sink into the sand a few inches from the parent plant and produce new plants. This plant may flower.

Sagittaria
(*Sagittaria gigantea*)

Sagittaria gigantea is one of the larger members of the genus Sagittaria. It looks much like the Vallisneria except that it is much thicker and stronger and will usually grow longer, sometimes reaching a length of 2 feet.

When planting Sagittaria, as well as other similar types of "crowned" plants, be sure that the crown (the place where the roots are fastened into the plant proper) is above the level of the sand. This will ensure maximum growth.

Sagittaria produces beautiful flowers and reproduces by sending out runners. These runners may be severed if there is need to separate the plants.

Hygrophila
(Hygrophila polysperma)

This new member of the group of aquarium plants comes from Asia and as yet is unequaled for rapid growth. Given sufficient light, it will soon fill up the aquarium. The author has had the Hygrophila grow right out of its tank and into the air some 3 or 4 inches.

The Hygrophila will grow well under almost any type of conditions and can survive extremes of temperatures and pH. New plants grow from the old by a series of roots dropping into the sand from the old plant. These roots may sprout from the parent plant as high as a foot above the sand level, though any joint is a possible crown.

Hygrophila should be planted low in the water, as it grows very quickly. Cuttings should be made every few weeks to keep the tank clear. The cuttings may be transplanted into another tank or merely stored in a jar of water.

This plant is not a true aquatic and may grow out into the air if the stem is strong enough. Since it will grow toward the light, be careful that it does not get dehydrated from getting too close to the reflector.

Nitella

Nitella is a type of stonewort, or Charales, one of the groups of plants forming a connecting link between the algae and flowering

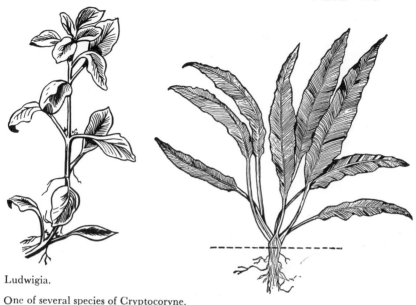

Ludwigia.

One of several species of Cryptocoryne.

plants. It looks much like emaciated Cabomba. It has a fine, long main stem from which very fine filaments protrude in all directions. It does not root and is excellent for use when spawning egg layers. Many fish will eat this plant, as it is very palatable.

Many schools use Nitella for protoplasmic demonstrations. It may be kept in a jar of water and will get along very well. Its growth is sometimes very rapid, and the more light the Nitella gets, the more dense it will be.

Amazon Sword Plant
(*Echinodorus intermedius*)

The most majestic of aquatic plants is truly the Amazon Sword. It is a crown-type plant that has thirty to forty leaves coming off the main stem, much as in stalks of celery. The plant looks so beautiful when it gets the proper light that it defies description. It is illustrated in the photograph on page 164.

Since it is a rather delicate plant, it must not be subjected to the treatment that plant-molesting fish like most Cichlids would give it. It grows to a height of 18 inches and may cover an area of 2 feet. It reproduces by runners, but also blossoms. Runners should be weighted into the sand.

The price of these plants is usually what makes them a rarity in the average home aquarium. About the cheapest mature Amazon available is five dollars.

Ludwigia

Though not a true water plant, Ludwigia has, nevertheless, found its way into those aquaria where light and richly fertilized sand is available.

Ludwigia, like Anacharis, tends to become very stringy and dies if sufficient light is not available. The beautiful red species which has been grown so successfully in Florida rarely maintains its luster in the environs of the Northeast.

The fact that Ludwigia does best in a rich soil culture bears out the fact that it is primarily a bog plant. Reproduction can be accomplished vegetatively, that is, the parent is divided into smaller plants. Cuttings planted in damp sand and humus will root quickly. The cutting can then be placed in the aquarium.

Cryptocoryne
(*Cryptocoryne sp.*)

The antithesis of Ludwigia is the Cryptocoryne. Cryptocoryne needs a minimum of light, and looks much like a terrestrial plant, with its long stem and broad green leaves, yellowish green on the under side. Planting is best done in a rich sand (containing some humus or earth). Many aquarists plant Cryptocoryne in 6-inch bulb pots and place these right in the sand. This will usually help keep earth or humus from making a nicely set up tank foul.

The plant reproduces by sending out shoots. Under optimum conditions, it sometimes flowers. As there are many species of Cryptocoryne, even plant taxonomists have trouble in differentiating them.

Floating Plants

Some floating plants have a place in the home aquarium. Many bubble-nest builders will use them in nest building, and other types of fish will nibble on their roots now and then.

About the most popular type of floating plant is Duckweed. It is merely a set of leaves, about three-eighths of an inch long, all attached at the center. A few species of this plant do exist, the *Lemna minor* and *Spirodela polyrhiza* being the most popular, but they are all quite similar.

Reproduction is vegetative. The roots may drop about an inch into the water; fish like to nibble on them. If given too much light, the Duckweeds will cover the top of an aquarium in a week. This will prohibit desirable top light from entering the tank through the surface and may also interfere with the elimination of carbon dioxide from the water.

Riccia is another type of floating plant that is useful for specific purposes, but grows so rapidly that it soon chokes out the sunlight that may enter from the top.

Riccia serves well for spawning purposes, but should be used with caution. Many enemies of fish like to lurk in the dark masses of this plant and await their prey.

Other types of floating plants, such as Salvinia, Lesser Bladderwort, and Water Hyacinth, have the same practical value as the aforementioned plants but are more delicate and expensive. Their uses are limited to bubble-nest builders and those types of fish that drop light eggs. The long roots of the Water Hyacinth may be a help to adhesive egg layers, but the expense and trouble of maintaining the Hyacinth are prohibitive.

Chapter 8
How to Keep Fish Healthy

Aquarium Conditions

Tropical fish, like most living organisms, are subject to various types of disease. Dr. Ross F. Nigrelli [1] of the New York Aquarium has made a very complete study of those factors which affect fish in captivity. Dr. Nigrelli lists the following factors which he believes account for the loss of fish in captivity:

1. CROWDING. A given aquarium will support only a certain number of fish before they will turn against each other in an effort to reduce their density. More carbon dioxide will also be present in the water and thus further add to the destruction. Diseases which are infectious will be more easily spread in the smaller tanks.

2. TEMPERATURE. Temperature fluctuations must be kept to a minimum. Though many fish have wide ranges of tolerance, successful adaptations to temperature changes require a long period of time. Higher temperatures may activate certain types of parasites, while lower temperatures might cause them to encyst (encase themselves and become inactive).

3. LIGHT. The fish generally kept in home aquaria are tolerant of a wide variety of light conditions. The quality—natural daylight, incandescent, or fluorescent—and quantity—providing they are not kept in total darkness or semidarkness for more than

[1] Nigrelli, R. F., "Causes of Diseases and Death of Fishes in Captivity," *Zoologica,* 28:203, 1943.

about two-thirds of the time—seem to make little difference to tropicals' well-being. The direction of light is important, however; most aquarists agree that artificial side lighting is detrimental. In order words, all artificial lighting should come from above the water's surface. Indeed, it is claimed that the best natural illumination also comes from above. It is widely believed that the principal reason fish in captivity spawn most frequently in the spring is because of the increasing length of daylight most apparent at that season. Certain types of flatworms (Trematoda) are phototropic (attracted to light) when in the larval stage. These trematodes, especially the Gyrodactylids, cause a very nasty disease of the skin and gills.

4. pH OF THE WATER. The most suitable pH (acidity or alkalinity) of the water is variable for individual types of fish. Marine fish require a pH of about 8.0, that is, slightly alkaline, while most tropicals require a pH of about 7.0, that is, neutral. Most species of fish, when kept in a tank of their own, will tend to keep the pH of the water at the most desirable level.

5. SPECIFIC GRAVITY OF THE WATER. Specific gravity (s.g.) may be defined as weight per unit volume as compared with an equal volume of water. The specific gravity of water is 1. Should water get heavier from an increase in dissolved substances it would increase some of the chemical changes that take place within the bodies of the fish. For example, their breathing would get more rapid. An increase in s.g. has a harmful effect upon many parasites in some instances.

6. FLOW AND AERATION OF WATER. Several gases are toxic to fish when they reach a certain concentration. Various fish require different amounts of aeration—to rid the water of gases such as carbon dioxide, hydrogen sulphide, and nitrogen.

7. METABOLIC WASTE PRODUCTS: Water contains many types of matter dissolved in it. Some of this material comes from the waste excreted by the fish. Certain types of this material are beneficial to some fish, but too strong a concentration is undoubtedly not good.

8. DIET. Many fish get poor diets and may suffer from various deficiencies. Liver and kidney troubles are frequent manifestations of vitamin deficiencies.

9. HANDLING. Many fish get scratched or lose a few scales when being handled. These openings are often sites of attack by harmful organisms.

10. PARASITES. Certain types of organisms attack the fish and live on them. Some parasites will attack only a specific fish, but there are many types of fish parasites that show no specificity. These types are the most dangerous.

Certain different types of ailments may be treated by the same methods, but there is definitely no "cure-all" for fish. Many types of medicines sold as cure-alls should be ignored. About the only medication that can be offered many ill fish is a bath in a gallon of water containing about 2½ tablespoons of plain household salt. The temperature of the water should then be raised so any encysted parasites may become active. It is wise to treat the whole tank with this salt treatment. Most diseases of fish are very infectious, and salt is the best type of nontoxic medicine to be recommended.

The widespread disease Ichthyophthirius, a type of protozoan parasite, commonly called the "Ich," is very successfully treated this way. The white spots, which usually indicate the presence of Ich, are the encysted parasite. A rise in temperature in this case is needed to enable the parasites to be free-swimming and thus become poisoned by the salt.

The author has been told by one of the greatest authorities on fish diseases that the only recommended remedy for fish ills is the salt treatment. Other treatments are usually toxic and may be more dangerous than the disease itself.

The new wonder drugs, the antibiotics, have finally successfully entered fish-cultural practices. Aureomycin has been found an excellent treatment for fungus and certain bacterial infections. A concentration of about 250 milligrams per 10 gallons of water is recommended. The whole dose of the drug is simply put into the water all at once. Other newly developed antibiotics also give promise of helping the aquarist both cure and prevent disease.

Professor Roberts Rugh [2] suggests the following precautions when dealing with fish:

It is almost safe to say that there is no reliable remedy for sick fish, no matter what the cause. Prevention is all-important, for really there is no cure! However, there are several simple rules to keep in mind:

1. Never add new fish to an old aquarium until they have been sterilized and quarantined for a few days. All new fish should be given a salt treatment, regardless of their source.

2. Provide separate aquaria for sick fish and isolate them as soon as there is any indication of trouble.

3. When shipping large numbers of fish, it is said that mortality will be reduced if a small amount of aspirin is added to the water (reasons unknown).

4. When sick fish are found in a regular aquarium, this aquarium should be put through a thorough process of cleaning and sterilization. Fish diseases are generally very contagious (for the fish!).

5. Overcrowding and overfeeding are probably the second and third most frequent causes of illness, the first being parasitization.

6. The chlorine in drinking (tap) water is a good bactericidal for human beings but harmful to fish. Chlorine will naturally evaporate from standing water if there is sufficient exposed surface, but warming or agitating the water will hasten the process.

Because sick fish, as previously explained, are usually weaker than healthy ones, they should be separated from the rest of the fish, even though they all may be getting the same treatment. To eliminate the trouble of temperature controls in a separate tank, a glass beaker filled with some of the water from the tank may be floated on the surface of the aquarium. A single small fish will do very well in such a small body of water, at least for a few days.

[2] Rugh, R., *Experimental Embryology*, Burgess Publishing Company, Minneapolis, Minnesota, 1948, p. 365.

Feeding

One of the greatest assets to a healthy tank is the food that the fish receive. How, as well as what, you feed your fish is a very important consideration. Most fish can safely be fed once a day, all they can eat in about ten minutes. Uneaten food should not be left to decay in the aquarium. Many more fish die from overfeeding, especially at the hands of beginners, than from starvation. Several important factors should be recognized when feeding fish:

1. SIZE OF FOOD PARTICLES. Make sure the particles are small enough for the fish to ingest.

2. VARIETY OF FOOD. Alternate different types of food.

3. QUANTITY OF FOOD. Larger fish, of course, need more food than smaller ones. Feed the fish small portions for about ten minutes. This will ensure a minimum waste of food. Some very active fish require several such feedings a day. More food should be given fish during the summer than winter. Also feed more food to fish in tanks that have more light than is normal.

It is up to the individual fancier, however, to judge the optimal feeding techniques and the varieties of food to be used.

Live Food

1. PLANTS. Such plants as algae, Duckweed, and lettuce are required in the diet of many fish (Scats, Mollies, Guppies, etc.). Many of the larger types of plants, such as Vallisneria, Cabomba, etc., also are good for fish to nibble on.

2. BRINE SHRIMP. These little marine animals are very handy. They are obtained in egg form and hatched in a solution of 6 tablespoons of salt to a gallon of water. The eggs should hatch out in two days at 75° F. The brine shrimp (*Artemia*) may be fed on plankton (salt-water infusion), algae, or lettuce, and raised to quite a size. These are excellent food for newborn fish.

Magnified brine shrimp (*Artemia*) showing egg sacs. These are excellent food for newborn fish. (*Courtesy General Biological Supply House.*)

For the hatching of brine shrimp eggs fill a few deep glass dishes with the salt solution to a depth not less than 1 inch. Add eggs in the proportion of one teaspoon to the gallon, or just roughly sprinkle some eggs over the surface of the water. Do not move the water after the eggs have been placed in it, as the eggs will usually stick to the sides of the dish.

After the culture has remained for two days, place a light at some part of the dish. The brine shrimp show positive phototropism, all congregating near the light, and are easily scooped up with a fine net.

It is impossible to pick up live brine shrimp without getting some eggs also. Snails usually take care of the uneaten eggs.

3. INFUSORIA. These include such organisms as amoebae, paramecia, blepharisma, rotifers, etc. They are made readily available in pill form, which may be cultivated into a strong infusion by the addition of a little lettuce. The Infusoria should be fed to newborn fry with an eyedropper. It is inadvisable to drop

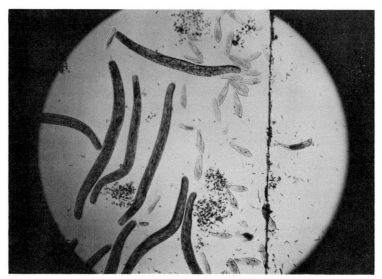

Infusoria (magnified). (*Courtesy General Biological Supply House.*)

the pill into the spawning tank, as certain pills will form a scum on the water surface.

4. DAPHNIA. These small relatives of shrimp, crabs, and lobsters are excellent food for every type of fish large enough to ingest them. Sifted Daphnia are excellent for fry. It is sometimes advisable to enter a few large Daphnia into the spawning tank so they may throw off young that will be small enough for the fry. Daphnia may be raised in beakers or battery jars with a minimum capacity of 2 pints. After about six adult Daphnia have been selected and placed in the jars, some Horlick's malted milk, dried, shredded lettuce, Infusoria, or hay should be placed in the jar for food. The Daphnia will reproduce in large numbers. The water may turn cloudy after the food is placed in it—perhaps because of the Infusoria—but this should not be a detriment as long as it does not turn moldy. The culture should be changed every month.

5. ENCHYTRAEIDS. These white worms are excellent food for

all types of fish. They may be chopped up into fine particles for the young fish. Cultures of white worms may be started with an inoculation of a few worms into some humus. This humus should be kept in a clay pot or wooden vessel. The temperature should be in the fifties, and the humidity should be very high. It may be a good idea to keep the culture in a dark, damp cellar. Food in the form of Horlick's malted milk, or dried milk, and bread of any kind is good. Cereal boiled in milk until it is pasty may also be inserted into the humus for food. The culture should stand about a month before being used.

6. TUBIFEX. These red worms are usually available all year round. They are very popular and nutritious for fish. Feedings of Tubifex may present two problems. First, Tubifex are sewer worms and are usually sold with much of the debris still intact in the culture. This decaying matter is liable to cloud up the culture if the worms are not thoroughly cleaned under cold running water. The second factor is that Tubifex may carry with them several types of parasite that are quite dangerous to tropical fish. This is another reason the red worms must be thoroughly cleaned.

These worms may be stored in the refrigerator for weeks in glass jars containing no less than 2 pints of water. The water in the jars should be changed daily. First, pour off as much water from the jar as possible. Then shoot a stream of water, as cold as possible, into the culture so the worms will all be separated. Allow the water to settle—the worms will sink to the bottom. Do this until the worms get very red and the water that comes off is clean. Then feed the fish a few worms, making sure that they are able to ingest the worms before they fall to the bottom of the tank. Should the worms fall to the bottom, they will burrow into the sand and be very difficult for the fish to pull out. Tubifex may be fed to the fish two or three times a week. Special feeding rings are available for this purpose.

In 1953 I wrote a booklet entitled *Tropical Fish as Pets*. Several of my associates challenged the wisdom of this title since fishes are not really "pets" in the sense that a horse, dog, or cat is actually "petable." Though I couldn't convince them that you can handle fishes in one way or another, it didn't make me change the title of the booklet. Since that time I have been very sensitive about training fishes; but, until now, I haven't had much luck.

Now the story changes. A few years ago a Chinese from Formosa (Taiwan) sent me samples of dried Tubifex. Within three weeks I had samples on my desk of five different types of dried Tubifex worms, all coming from Formosa or Japan. The fishes ignored most of them.

Laughingly, Bernie Duke, who runs Gulf Fish Farms in Palmetto, Florida, said, "Herb, you need catnip for your fish food." He laughed. I laughed. I started thinking.

Scientifically, we know that certain substances increase fishes' appetites and attract them to investigate certain "odors" which might be food. I worked with a few of them and finally found my "fish nip." It is similar to the "taste odor" in the German fish food known as "TetraMin," but is distinctive in that it is an all-meat product, very high in protein.

Once fishes discover it in an aquarium, they tear it apart with such vigor that you would think that they hadn't eaten for a month. After almost a year of testing, I discovered that I could raise Angel fish, *Bettas, Corydoras,* all the live bearers, most of the Tetras, and even African water frogs, solely on a diet of these freeze-dried Tubifex worms. The food was great! We called them "Miracle Worms."

Further refinements in the processing made possible the following characteristics:

a. If allowed to soak in a glass of clear water, the worms will float for days and will not cloud or discolor the water. The food is also odorless.

b. As the worms pick up moisture, they expand and look exactly like live Tubifex worms.

The new food described here is relished by virtually every species of tropical fish. Here we see cardinal tetras tearing greedily into some of the food which has been stuck to the front glass of an aquarium. (*Photo by Dr. Herbert R. Axelrod.*)

Fishes that have been fed the freeze-dried worms zero in on it from all directions the moment it is put in the tank. Amateur fish photographers need only focus on the glass where they will put the food to be assured of perfect shots. There won't be a fish in the tank that doesn't swim into range. (*Photo by Dr. Herbert R. Axelrod.*)

c. When pressed against the inside glass of an aquarium, they adhere, and the fishes can be fed so that every bit they eat can be observed. This prevents overfeeding since you can easily remove any uneaten bits of worms. Overfeeding is the single greatest "disaster" than can foul the tank (and enthusiasm) of any beginner.

d. It is so nutritious that it can bring almost every known aquarium fish into breeding condition. This food and brine shrimp are perfect diets for all fishes . . . bar none.

e. The fishes enjoy eating it so much, as evidenced by their voracious attacks on it, that they become tame and will eagerly pick at it from between your fingers. I have proven this with nocturnal Catfish, Mollies, Gouramis, Angel Fish, Cardinal Tetras, and most Cichlids.

Here is the proper method to train your fishes. For the first three days merely affix a small piece of *Miracle* Tubifex worms to the center of your aquarium glass (or just drop it into the aquarium if you don't want to get your hands wet). Let your fishes develop a taste for it. It may take them five or ten minutes actually to attack it since the food emits powerful "odors" and they may be "suspicious." Once they have acclimated themselves to the worms, don't feed them for one day. The next day they will almost eat the freeze-dried Tubifex from between your fingers.

7. MOSQUITO "LARVAE." Immature mosquitoes are fine food for the tropicals. These wrigglers are actually the pupae, not the larvae, of the mosquito. They may be purchased, or gathered from swampy pools along with Daphnia. The only objection to these larvae is that should they metamorphose before they are eaten, you are liable to have a houseful of mosquitoes.

8. EARTHWORMS. These familiar organisms are ideal for large types of fish such as the Cichlids. They may be chopped up and fed to the smaller tropicals. Bloodworms and sandworms also fall into the same category.

9. DROSOPHILA. These little fruit flies may be obtained from any high school or college that offers a course in biology or from

a biological supply house. A certain mutant type, called "vestigial," has very small wings and cannot fly. If a male and female Drosophila are placed in a small cream container, or similar jar, with a piece of banana or other type of nutrient, they will reproduce very profusely.

10. MICROWORMS. Imported from Europe, these newly discovered threadlike worms, technically called *Anguillula silusiae,* are about an eighth of an inch long and make excellent food for all types of newly hatched fish. Young live bearers also relish this food. The original cost of starting the culture is about the only expense necessary to have a year-round supply of live food for all the young that would be spawned in any home aquarium. They may be purchased at any large tropical-fish store. The best type of container for their quickly growing culture is a refrigerator jar. Most purchased cultures come in such a container. They can be kept at room temperature, 68° F.

Since most of the microworms are females, and reproduce by giving off living young, the food supply diminishes rapidly and new food is required; owing to its contents, the food supply should be changed every two weeks, in any case. The usual mixture that has been found successful is a water mixture of three parts Pablum to one part yeast. This paste should be placed about one-half inch deep in the refrigerator jars. The worms will not be able to eat all the culture medium before it turns sour. Care must be exercised that the medium does not dehydrate. Some people tape the edges of the refrigerator jar to prevent the loss of water through evaporation. This is a good idea, also, because the worms seem to fare very well with a limited air supply.

Separation of the worms from the culture medium is no problem since the worms do not actually live in the medium but rather prefer to stay on the sides of the glass near the surface of the culture. They may be fed to the fish directly after being scraped off the sides with a finger or knife.

Starting a new culture is usually done by adding a "fingerful" of worms to a freshly prepared culture dish. This dish, containing the same food as the old, should be started a few days before you intend to throw out the old medium—a culture should not be kept more than two weeks—so you will always have an abundance of microworms for the young fish.

Prepared Foods and Formulas

There are many types of prepared food which, if interspersed with other types, are very beneficial to captive fish. Listed below are probably the most nutritious ones. Caution should be exercised, however, to avoid being too repetitious with these foods.

1. Ant "eggs."
2. Cereals—the smaller grained ones.
3. Eggs—chopped up yolk of hard-boiled eggs.
4. Potato—boiled thoroughly and broken up into fine pieces.
5. Fish—all sorts of raw fish may be chopped into small pieces and fed sparingly to all types of fish. Frozen fillet of flounder is easy to keep. Merely cut off a small piece every day and feed with a little dry food. Cichlids do very well on this diet.
6. Shrimps—fresh, shelled, and chopped into fine pieces, or dropped into the tank on pieces of string so they may be pulled out after ten or fifteen minutes. Care should be used to remove them soon enough, for shrimp will cloud the water if left in the tank for too long a period.
7. All sorts of dry prepared foods for sale in pet shops and other stores. They are all usually satisfactory, but they should not be used exclusively.

Gordon's Formula [3]

This requires a pound of liver, 20 tablespoons of Pablum or Ceravim, and 1 tablespoon of salt. Cut the liver into one-half-inch

[3] *The Care and Breeding of Laboratory Animals,* John Wiley & Sons, New York, 1950, p. 376.

pieces and remove all the sinewy material. Add an equivalent weight of water. Grind the liver into a mash (a Waring Blendor is excellent for this purpose), and then drain through a fine sieve. Then add Pablum or Ceravim slowly to the liver to form a thick paste. Mix this meal in well, seeing that there are no lumps. The salt may be added during this process. Now place the mixture in small glass jars. Place the jars in a pot of water and boil. Put the covers on the jars, but do not screw them down or the jars may burst from the expanding gases. When the water has boiled, turn off the heat and allow the jars to cool with the water for half an hour. Screw the caps on, if possible, as soon as the heat is turned off. When the jars have been thoroughly cooled, they may be placed in the refrigerator and safely stored for a month or so. All fish seem to have a hearty appetite for this mixture, so feed it sparingly, allowing the fish to eat only small amounts at a time.

Chapter 9
Appliances—Use and Repair

The most important consideration to be given an appliance is its usefulness in the aquarium. As there is an infinite number of appliances which can be purchased to add to the complexity—or simplicity—of aquarium management, we shall explain the operation of only those few which are a necessity to every aquarium.

A necessary requirement for every appliance is that it be made of a noncorrosive material. Stainless steel, glass, and certain plastics are the safest materials to put in an aquarium. If an appliance is not available in a safe material, do without it.

Thermometers

Thermometers measure the temperature of the water. Most thermometers for use in the aquarium are filled with mercury, colored alcohol, or colored water. The best is the mercury thermometer. As accuracy is obviously the criterion of a good thermometer, it would be profitable to analyze here what makes a thermometer accurate.

A thermometer works on the principle of an expanding liquid. A calibrated glass tube is used to measure this expansion. Mercury is the most accurate liquid for this purpose, as it expands the most evenly with every rise in temperature. It is obvious that the longer the thermometer, the more accurately it can be read.

Aquarium thermometers are sold in different models. Some are filled with air and float. Others are weighted with lead shot and stand on the bottom of the tank. Still another model is fastened to the side of the aquarium by a suction cup. The easiest to read without removal from the water is the one fastened to the side of the tank, though the standing type can also be set to allow for easy reading.

Since the temperature of a large tank of water is not uniform throughout—it may be 10 degrees warmer at the top of the water than at the bottom—it may be wise to have both a floating thermometer and a standing thermometer. Aeration helps to maintain an even temperature throughout the aquarium.

Do not use boiling water, or even very hot water, to clean the algae off a thermometer, or the thermometer will undoubtedly break. Aquarium thermometers are usually set between 50° and 100° F.; the temperature of boiling water is 212° F. To get the algae off, merely run some steel wool over it a few times and rinse it in some water that has a temperature in the tolerable range of the thermometer.

Most aquarium thermometers are accurate to within about 2 degrees. When comparing the temperature of two or more tanks, use the same thermometer and measure the temperature at the same depth of water.

Thermostats

Since the majority of tropical fish comes from waters where the temperature is rather constantly above 75° F., you must see that the temperature of the water in your aquarium never drops below that point. A thermostat, composed of a bimetallic strip that bends backward and forward with each rise and fall of the temperature, will make this easy. This bending action can be utilized to make and break an electrical circuit. An electrical heater in the circuit will go on when the circuit is completed. As soon as the

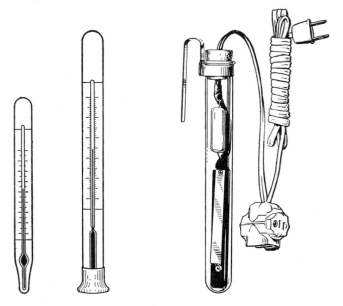

LEFT: The floating and the standing types of thermometers.

RIGHT: Thermostat with triple-head plug for attaching heaters.

water in which the thermostat is located reaches a predetermined temperature, the bimetallic strip bends away from its contact and breaks the circuit, thus shutting off the heater. Almost all thermostats can be regulated by a set screw that moves closer, or farther away, from the bimetallic strip as it is turned. By regulating the distance from the screw to the strip the temperature at which you want the thermostat to operate can be regulated. Most thermostats fail to operate because of corrosion on the point of contact between the thermostat and the set screw. It is advisable to check on this factor every few months. Sometimes it is good to run a nail file over the contacts to make sure that conducting surfaces are in contact. Of course, the thermostat has to be readjusted after such a treatment.

Many thermostats are located in the same unit as the heater, which is obviously not too good an arrangement, as the heat from the heater will have more effect on the thermostat than the temperature of the more distant water. Thermostatic units which are located separately from the heater, besides being most advantageous, are usually most economical, since more than one heater can be operated from a single thermostatic unit. When operating such a system, it is advisable to use a thermostat in the smallest tank as far from the heater as possible, as smaller bodies of water are liable to more drastic temperature changes. When operating a great number of heaters from a single thermostatic unit, the wattage rating of the thermostat should be checked. Thermostats are all rated at the maximum safe load they can carry, and if overloaded, they will burn out. When overloaded, the spark which jumps across from the bimetallic strip to the set screw will be so hot that it will actually weld the two units together. This can be most disastrous since the thermostat will not be able to turn off the heater and the fish will ordinarily be cooked to death. To calculate whether the load on the thermostat is safe, add up the total wattage of the heaters and be sure that it does not add up greater than the wattage rating of the thermostat.

Many thermostats are built with condensers (capacitors) to eliminate static or interference in radio and television sets. These capacitors are easily added to any unit that does not already have one. Any radio store will sell them at less than a dime apiece. They may be easily installed by placing them across the circuit at any point. If you are skeptical about your ability to make this minor adjustment, let your radio man do it.

The quality of a thermostat can generally be determined by the material of which the points of contact are composed. Silver contacts are usually the only low-priced acceptable contacts.

Heaters

Closely allied to thermostats, as seen from the discussion above, are the heaters. These are essentially small electric coils enclosed in a conduction jacket. This jacket is usually made of Pyrex glass.

A single-tube heater-thermostat.

The Pyrex-glass test tubes make the best all-around jackets, though chrome jackets are now becoming popular.

It is of the utmost importance that no water be allowed to seep into the heater. If it does, it evaporates when the heater goes on; the water vapor then builds up great pressure in the closed container and is very liable to explode. The pressure is sometimes great enough to blow out the sides of an aquarium.

Of the different kinds of heaters, the submersible type is the most advantageous, in principle, although it is most susceptible to explosion. (Should it fail to operate, take it back to the store, as the waterproofing is not guaranteed if the heater has been tampered with.) It heats the water at the bottom of the tank, thus allowing convection currents to heat the tank more evenly than if the surface of the water is heated. Make sure that the heater does not get buried in the sand. Stratification takes place when the top of the water is heated and the bottom is at a much lower temperature. This is a dangerous situation which jeopardizes the health of the fish in the aquarium. Many people advise the use of two heaters, one the regular immersion type, the other the

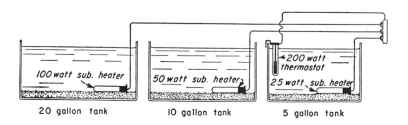

100 watt sub. heater

20 gallon tank

50 watt sub. heater

10 gallon tank

←200 watt thermostat

25 watt sub. heater

5 gallon tank

Satisfactory way to set up heater and thermostatic unit. Note that a 200-watt thermostat is used, even though the total load is only 175 watts.

Thermostat and heater should be as far from each other as possible.

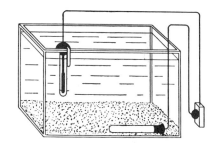

submersible type. This tends to stabilize and equalize the temperature in the tank. Both heaters should operate from the same thermostat.

To calculate the wattage heater necessary for a given tank, allow 5 watts for every gallon of water to be heated. Thus, in a 10-gallon tank, a 50-watt heater should be used. Should a lower wattage heater be used, there would be danger that the heater would not give off enough heat to raise the temperature to that required by the thermostat. This would mean that the heater would burn continuously, thus greatly reducing its life span. Using too powerful a heater is just as bad; it will go off and on every few seconds and probably burn out the thermostat.

When hanging an immersion-type, nonsubmersible heater in an aquarium, be sure that the heater is only as far in the water as will safely ensure against the admittance of water into the jacket. On the other hand, the danger of having too much of the heater exposed to the air is apparent when you consider the conductivity of water as compared with that of air. Naturally the part exposed to air will get very hot since air is a very poor conductor of heat and will not cool the glass to any great degree; on the other hand the water will cool off the bottom part of the jacket, thus creating a drastic difference in temperature between the top of the jacket and the bottom. Most glass jackets would crack under the strain. If the heater has a built-in thermostat, the thermostatic unit will probably be located near the top of the heater. Again the consequences are apparent should the heater not be deep enough in the water.

Air Pumps

The advantages of aeration of water are twofold. First, it is helpful in ridding the water of the harmful carbon dioxide which, when allowed to accumulate, has such a detrimental effect on most fish. Second, it serves the very useful purpose of aiding in the circulation of the water, thus ensuring a more even distribution of heat.

The mechanism for the supply of air is the commercial air pump, of which several different types are available to the aquarist. In the piston type of pump, air is compressed and forced through the air lines, usually rubber or plastic tubing, to run the air stones or filters. The piston-type pump has two cycles, the compression stroke and the intake stroke. When the piston is pushed down into the cylinder, the air is compressed, thus the compression stroke. When the piston is raised up, it sucks in air by creating a vacuum in the cylinder. The cylinder is fitted with a certain type of valve that is closed during the compression stroke and open to admit air during the intake stroke.

Another type of pump is the vibrating-membrane type. A rubber membrane that vibrates quite rapidly takes the place of the cylinder-piston arrangement just described. Most of the vibrating-membrane type pumps have lower capacities than do the more conventional piston types. The rubber membranes need replacing after a period of six months to a year, and there is a definite air loss when slight cracks develop in the rubber membrane because of the incessant vibration. Most manufacturers have facilities for the replacement of these parts and it is the wisest policy to return the pumps to the manufacturer for adjustment and repair. The cost is usually trivial. Don't, under any circumstances, try to replace the membrane yourself!

The air pressure built up by most vibrating-membrane pumps runs between 3 and 6 pounds per square inch. Naturally, the greater the pressure the greater the number of outlets the pump can maintain.

In general, insofar as price alone is concerned, the cheaper pumps are vibrating-membrane types. The principal objection to this type of pump is the noise that it makes. It has the advantage of being cheaper to buy, cheaper to operate, and it is usually sufficient for two or three small tanks.

The proper arrangement of air stones, filters, and escape valve is most important in utilizing the full capacity of the pump. The arrangement suggested in the diagram is probably the easiest and most efficient.

It is sometimes very desirable to calculate the cost of operation of a certain pump or other electrical appliance for a given period of time. This is easily accomplished merely by finding out the rate of electricity in your neighborhood. In New York City, the rates run about four cents per kilowatt hour. That means a 1,000-watt appliance can be operated for one hour at a cost of four cents. The formula is as follows:

$$\text{Cost} = \frac{\text{wattage} \times \text{number of hours} \times \text{rate per kw hour}}{1000}$$

Not all appliances give the wattage. All, however, must give enough information so that wattage can be easily figured out.

$$\text{Wattage} = \text{Amperage} \times \text{Voltage}$$

where

$$\text{Amperage} \times \text{Ohms} = \text{Voltage}$$

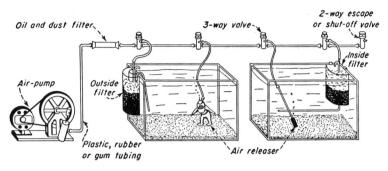

Air line system should be as simple as possible.

Some things to look for in a good pump are: low wattage (less than 40 watts), a year's guarantee, easy to repair, easy to lubricate, static free (equipped with a condenser), beltless, replaceable rings for pistons (felt or leather being best), noiseless, and great output (in cubic inches of air).

Filters

Filtration of the water is rapidly gaining the recognition it deserves. Aside from aeration, filtration is the best aid to a "balanced" aquarium. Not only does it eliminate solid waste particles floating in the water but, with the use of activated charcoal, it helps to remove the harmful gases dissolved in the water. Filtration is also very useful in aiding the circulation of water.

The mechanics of filtration are easily understood. A filter system is set up so that water is forced to pass through a straining device—usually glass wool or sand, or both—to remove solid debris, and then on through some activated charcoal to remove the dissolved gases.

The advantages of outside and inside filters are open to debate. About the only great advantage the inside filter has over the outside filter is that should the filter fall from the tank or develop

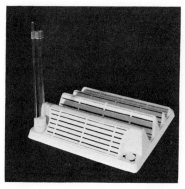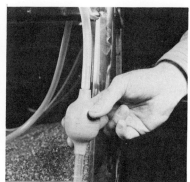

LEFT: A modern undergravel filter.

RIGHT: Rubber-bulb siphons are very handy for cleaning your aquarium.

a leak, the water will not continue to run out, as in the outside filter, until the syphon loses contact with the water. The inside filter, however, occupies more space than the outside filter, and will crowd the aquarium a little and be rather unsightly.

Cleaning of the sand and glass wool is easy. Merely run hot water over the sand for a few minutes to get all the dirt and debris out of it. The glass wool should be spread apart and the dirt rubbed out. To recharge the activated charcoal, you need only to cook it on the stove for fifteen or twenty minutes. Filter stems and return stems should be cleaned periodically with a brush just for this purpose.

Under-gravel filtration, a principle which was responsible for a major boom in the aquarium hobby, was invented by Norman Hovlid. Hovlid founded the Miracle Filter Company to manufacture his wonderful invention. The Hovlid principle is in placing a flat plastic tray under the gravel. The tray has about a one-fourth-inch space between it and the bottom of the aquarium. Water is drawn through the gravel by means of the Miracle filter and returned to the top of the aquarium.

The great advantage of this type of filtration is that there are no messy filters to be cleaned and glass wool changed. It also keeps the water much clearer than normal filters and the water never needs changing unless it is polluted.

Syphoning Tubes

As much of the debris—dead snails, leaves, feces, and uneaten food—is usually too heavy to float or be suspended in the water, the filter will not be able to gather it up. The auxiliary tank cleaner to be used to remove this heavy debris is the syphon.

Originally, most syphons were constructed primarily for the removal of water, but recently new types of syphons have been placed on the market to syphon the dirt out of the tank. Special angle glass and glass valves have been devised that allow for the picking up of the lighter debris without disturbing the heavier sand.

Those syphons which are known as "dip tubes" work on the syphon principle but are not continuous. When you place your finger over the top of a straw and then put the straw deep into some water, you notice that the water rushes into the straw as soon as you release the finger from the top. This principle was utilized in constructing a widemouth "straw" to pick up bottom debris. Obviously the dip tube must be emptied after each insertion.

Fish Nets

This is one accessory that apparently seems rather insignificant to the average aquarist. Many people fail to realize the importance of using a proper-sized net to catch fish. Small nets make the actual capture of the fish more difficult, besides increasing the danger to the fish itself. It is much easier to damage a fish in a small net than in a large one. It is also much easier for a fish to jump out of a small net than from the larger, deeper size.

The correct size of net should be at least 1 inch longer than the

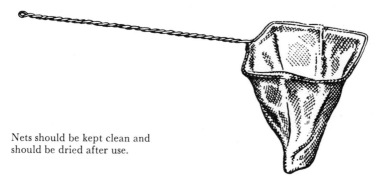

Nets should be kept clean and
should be dried after use.

fish. Widths run accordingly. If one net is all the budget allows,
buy the largest practical. Even small Guppies should be handled
in 3-inch nets.

Most nets for tropical fish are made of Brussels net. Brussels
net is a strong, porous material that makes excellent netting. The
gauze netting, being more closely knit than the Brussels, is usually
used in the cheaper nets.

Lately nylon nets have become popular. The only objection
to them is that they do not allow the water to pass through very
easily and thus they hinder the aquarist in the capture of fast-
moving fish. Nylon nets are excellent for the capture of brine
shrimp or small Daphnia. Fry and Daphnia nets are specially
made of a very fine material.

As the frames of good nets are usually of strong, stainless wire,
they always seem to outlast the netting. It is rather easy to cut out
a piece of white cotton, or purchase regular netting, and construct
a new net. However, nets are so inexpensive that it hardly pays
to make one's own.

pH Test Kits

It is sometimes of the utmost importance to check the pH of the
water. This is sometimes measured so accurately that a simple
exposure to air will make a marked difference. That kind of cal-
culation, however, is not necessary at all for the aquarist. You

pH cannot be accurately estimated and must be measured with a pH kit.

need only be interested in fluctuations of a unit or so. Neutral pH is 7.0. Acidity runs from 0 to 7.0; alkalinity runs from 7.0 to 14.0. The maximum tolerance for tropical fish for any period of time is from about 6.0 to 8.0.

Certain indicators, such as bromthymol blue, litmus, phenolphthalein, change color with a change in pH. These indicators can be so calibrated that by comparing the amount of change of any given dye—this comparison is usually accomplished by a color chart—you can tell the acidity or alkalinity of the water.

Chemicals are available separately, or a complete pH Test Kit may be purchased. For more accurate measurements, electrical pH test meters are available.

Buffer solutions may be purchased to aid in the alteration and stabilization of the pH. Care should be exercised that the buffer does not harm the fish.

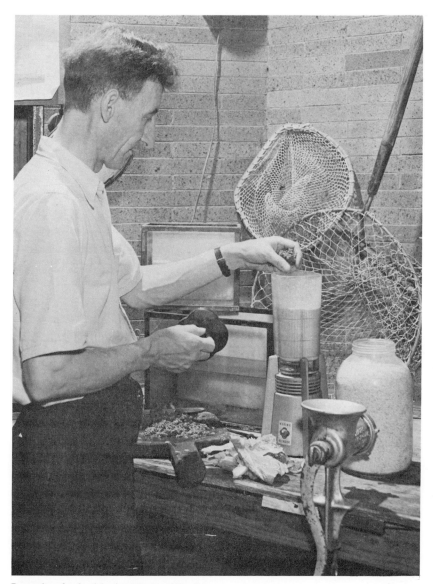

Preparing food with the Waring Blendor.

Planting Tongs and Snips

Special tongs are available to assist in the planting of new vegetation after the tank is already set. These tongs are useful in deep tanks and in tanks where dangerous fish, such as the Piranha, are kept. They should be so constructed that they will not damage the plants. They should also be rustproof.

Planting snips are used to trim plants. They are merely long-handled scissors. Again, they should be rustproof, as should every aquarium accessory.

Waring Blendor

Credit for the invention of the Waring Blendor goes to a famous musician, Fred Waring, who is said to have developed it when he was forced to subsist on pulverized food. Since most of the commercially prepared foods were rather distasteful, Waring invented a type of blade set in a large cup over a small electric motor. The foods were placed in the cup and ground to a very fine texture.

Use of the Waring Blendor started to be of interest to aquarists when Dr. Myron Gordon first developed his formula which called for the liquefaction of calf's liver. Since then many other foods are being prepared by the Blendor. Young Gouramis are being well fed on the egg-yolk infusion which got its start when it was broken up into dust-fine particles in the Blendor.

Chapter 10
The Salt–water Aquarium

The magnificent color of some small marine tropical fish has made many an eye turn toward the possibility of maintaining a salt-water aquarium.

The size of such an aquarium should be no less than 10 gallons; smaller tanks become foul very easily. In selecting a tank for a marine aquarium, it should be taken into account that salt water is a powerful destroyer of metals, and that therefore it is of utmost importance that no metal should come in contact with the salt water. The salt water also has an effect on some types of aquarium cement. It is advisable to protect the cement by covering it with black asphaltum varnish.

Precautions should be taken to ensure that the reflector is protected from the spray of salt water possibly caused by the air stone. Complete top coverage by a glass plate is most advisable for this reason. This not only protects the reflector and its working parts, but also keeps evaporation down to a minimum.

Since the aquarium is to be marine, it should be natural that the hobbyist acquire sea water. However, there are various formulas for artificial sea water offered as substitutes.

Since plants, other than seaweeds, are not common to salt water and since these do not thrive in tanks, no plants should be introduced into the aquarium.

As all uneaten particles of food must be syphoned off each day,

Four-eyed Butterfly Fish (*Chaetodon capistratus*), a marine favorite.

Clown Fish (*Amphiprion percula*) is found near coral reefs in the western Pacific and Indian oceans. It is one of the few marine fishes that has been bred in aquaria.

it is easier to have as little decorative material in the aquarium as possible. It is better to do without sand, but should you choose to include it, use very fine sand, so that all particles of food may be easily reached in syphoning. All seashells and coral should be thoroughly boiled before being allowed to have a place in the marine aquarium. Sometimes after use, the seashells and coral will tend to become discolored and lose their milk-white appearance. To be brought back to their original color the shells must be bleached. Any regular household bleach may be used. Simply take the shell out and place it in a container of hot, fresh water. Add the bleach. Allow it to soak for a day or so, and then allow a day for drying. After the shell is completely dry, boil it again in plain water and replace it in the aquarium.

The temperature should be maintained at about 70° F. Marine fish cannot tolerate as much temperature fluctuation as can fresh-water tropicals. In heating the aquarium, again, be sure that there is no metal touching the water. *Do not use chrome heaters.*

Filtration and aeration are practically a necessity in the marine aquarium, though aeration is even more important that filtration. Again, precautions about the metal-water contacts should be taken. *Replace all water that has evaporated with tap water.* Do not keep refilling with sea water, as too great a salt content will result. The salts in sea water never evaporate.

Marine tropicals need live food, the best being young Mollies and Guppies. It is not a difficult matter to acclimate Mollies and Guppies to salt-water conditions. Keep the Mollies and Guppies in a tank for five weeks, adding an ounce of salt (Turk Island) each week per gallon of water. After this time, the fish are ready to be placed in the marine aquarium. As well as the Guppies and Mollies, most marine fish will usually eat small quantities of Tubifex, white worms, Daphnia, and bits of fish and clam. Brine shrimp are excellent food for marine tropicals and they will live long enough in the salt water to be eagerly eaten by the fish.

Be sure that all leftover food is removed from the marine aquarium.

Young salt-water Angel Fish. (*Courtesy General Biological Supply House.*)

When faced with treating the diseases of marine fish, use fresh water and permanganate instead of the salt treatment. Remove the fish from the tank as soon as any discomfort is obvious.

Salt-water Fish and Invertebrates

SEA HORSES (*Hippocampus* species). Although not the most beautiful of marine animals, the sea horses have an admiring public. Their interesting antics give them a distinct personality, and their odd appearance makes them a favorite with all children.

Different species of sea horses vary in size up to 12 inches in

Sea horses (*Hippocampus hudsonius.*)

length. Their tails are prehensile, that is, they are adapted for grasping or wrapping around objects. Sea horses normally swim by movements of the dorsal fin, but usually remain in a position with their tails coiled about some seaweed or coral.

Reproduction in the sea horse is interesting. In the spring or summer, the female produces about a hundred or so eggs, which she places in the male's belly pouch. This process may take a few days. The male then incubates the eggs for forty to fifty days until the young, with remnants of yolk sac, are "born." The young are free-swimming at this time. The young are exceedingly difficult to raise since they are not fast and will only take live food, brine shrimp and Daphnia being the best. Adult sea horses need live food in the form of good-sized brine shrimp, Daphnia, Guppies, Mollies, and worms.

SEA ANEMONES. These animals are really a peculiarity. There are about one thousand different types, most of them not being free-swimming, but attaching themselves by means of a broad sucker foot. Most anemones have about ninety-six tentacles, many containing stings. It is usually practical to place these animals on a sloping slate in the tank to help them move about freely. If there is loose sand in the tank, they have difficulty traveling over it and so usually traverse about the sides of the aquarium. Removing them from the sides of the aquarium is usually accomplished by keeping a steady pressure on them until they release; a razor blade may also help.

Sea anemones should be fed pieces of raw meat or fish. The small pieces should be dropped into their tentacles.

Most marine fish are rather scarce and are found only at fish dealers' occasionally. The Bibliography (p. 285) will be helpful in getting information on any particular species.

Chapter 11
How Fish Get Their Names[1]
By Dr. Myron Gordon

When a visitor comes to see the fish in my laboratory aquarium, the first thing he usually does is to ask me: "What kind of fish are they?"

"That small rainbow-colored one," I may say to him, "is *Lebistes reticulatus,* originally from Trinidad and northern South America. This red one with the black spots is *Xiphophorus maculatus* from British Honduras. That one with the long, green, swordlike tail is *Xiphophorus hellerii* from the streams flowing down the snow-capped peak of Mount Orizaba in Mexico."

The geographical place names may be familiar to the visitor but the scientific names of the fish usually stump him. If I substitute the common names of the fish and say "Guppies, Platyfish, and Swordtails," my guest smiles knowingly. Visitors and aquarists often ask why do scientists use the cumbersome, less familiar name *Lebistes reticulatus* when "Guppy" will do?

Scientific names of animals do have an important use. They are part of the grand system of zoological bookkeeping, technically known as "classification." In this gigantic arrangement of all the world's organisms (the names alone fill more than

---

[1] "How Fishes Get Their Names" appeared first in *The Fish Culturist* in 1932. Subsequently, in somewhat enlarged form, it was republished in *The Aquarium,* and in *The Aquarium Journal.* This new, revised version appeared first in *Water Life and Aquaria World,* n.s. 5:76–78 April–May, 1950. This revised version has had changes made to reflect currently correct nomenclature.

sixty volumes, and one or two new volumes appear every year), all the animals, living or extinct, large or microscopic, aquatic, terrestrial, arboreal, or subterranean, are listed in terms of species, genus, tribe, family, order, class, and phylum. These categories are intended to indicate the degree of relationship they bear to each other and to their position in the scale of evolution.

Zoologist's Classification

The fundamental basis for classifying animals in various groups, each group varying in relative position, each position indicating the closeness of relationship, is the structure of the body. The zoologist, after years of training, can place newly discovered forms by studying the resemblances in body structure. Sometimes only a fragment of a bone or tooth is sufficient for him to locate its owner's place in the all-inclusive zoological catalogue. Everybody has a special working vocabulary in his own profession or business, and nobody can learn a trade well without learning the names of the tools or the technical terms he must use.

It took biologists a long time to simplify their present-day scientific terminology. For example, the eighteenth-century ichthyologist, Petrus Artedi, found a curio in the form of a dried fish in Nag's Head Inn in London. He described it, saying it was like a little box, triangular in shape and with two horns in front and two spines under the tail. The systematist Artedi translated the description of the fish curio into Latin and produced this prayer-like sounding phrase: *Ostracion triangulatus duobus aculeis in fronte et totiden in imo ventre subcaudalesque binis.* For a while that Latinized verbal picture was the scientific name of the common horned Trunkfish. In 1758, Carolus Linnaeus streamlined this cumbersome appellation to the first two words, *Ostracion triangulatus,* and initiated the current practice of nomenclature in biology.

The common name of a fish or plant, or any other living or

extinct organism, serves a purpose, but often it has limited use-fulness. When a biological-research director took charge of one of the New England states' fishery problems, he found men in his Fish and Game Department indiscriminately transplanting "pin-minnows" and other kinds of small forage fish from a locality of great abundance to places where they were needed more. When one of these fish-game wardens was asked to pick out pin-minnows from a random collection in his net, he picked out fish belonging to *four* distinct species. He did not realize that pin-minnows were not all alike and that some of them, like the Fall-fish, grow to 2 or 3 pounds in weight. When Fallfish minnows are transferred to the cold-water habitats of the native brook trout, they become the trout's most serious competitor for the available food supply. Needless to say, the practice of indiscrim-inate transplanting of pin-minnows was stopped.

Scientists have been debating the problem of these complex names for a century. The systematists have tried constantly to improve their method for classifying and cataloguing the thou-sands of different kinds of organisms. An inventory of the world's living things must be universal in scope and written in a universal language.

How the Guppy Got Its Name

In 1850 Herr Peters in Germany obtained and described a small fish from Venezuela which he considered new to science. He was privileged to attach to it a new name which was *Poecilia reticu-lata*. Consider these two words in this new technical name for a moment. *Poecilia* was a word coined by M. Bonaparte, the grandnephew of the world-famous Napoleon, over one hundred years ago (1838). A free translation of *Poecilia* may be given as "little variegated fish." Henceforth, all new discoveries of fish which had the published characteristics of that fish had to bear this stamp.

Peters thought that his new fish was related to *Poecilia* and so designated it. But to distinguish his fish from those previously described he gave it the specific name of *reticulata,* which is not very different from our English word "reticulated," or netted. Of the two words, *Poecilia reticulata,* the fist, the generic name, and the second, the specific name, together constitute the scientific name. This method of naming a new species is technically termed "binomial nomenclature"—a practice followed universally by biologists. A set of rules has been established known as the "International Rules of Nomenclature." They are rigidly enforced.

Two years after Herr Peters' description appeared, Signor de Filippi in Italy described another small fish which had been sent to him from the West Indian Island of Barbados. Whether de Filippi read Peters' account or not is not known, but de Filippi thought he, too, had a new fish previously unknown to science. He named it *Lebistes poeciloides.* The generic name, *Lebistes,* was not previously used and informs us that in de Filippi's estimation this fish is only distantly related to the other Poeciliid fish. The word *Lebistes* refers to a kettle or pot, probably from the rotund appearance of a gravid female. *Poeciloides* means like a Poeciliid, or small fish.

Again, in 1866, Albert Guenther, in England, looking over the specimens of fish sent to the British Museum by a naturalist from northeastern South America, separated out a few which he regarded as being different from any he had previously known. Guenther thought this new fish was related to *Girardinus,* a new genus of Cuban fish described by Señor Poey in 1855 at Havana. Poey created the word "Girardinus" in honor of Charles Girard, a famous American ichthyologist.

As a compliment to their discoverer in the field, Lechmere Guppy, ichthyologist Albert Guenther named this fish *Girardinus guppii.* It was under this scientific name that the fish was brought to the attention and delight of the German and English aquarists.

The latter part of this name, *guppii,* has persisted even to this day. It is no longer its scientific name but a popular one. Guenther paid his friend Guppy a lasting compliment indeed, for the latter's name is heard everywhere—although people who use it frequently do not realize its significance and history.

Because this little fish varies greatly in coloration and fin structure, it is not surprising that each of the above ichthyologists thought he had something different and new. For a time, the fish known to aquarists as the "Guppy" had three scientific names, as follows: *"Poecilia reticulata,"* given in 1859 by Peters in Germany; *"Lebistes poeciloides,"* given in 1861 by de Filippi in Italy; and *"Girardinus guppii,"* given in 1866 by Guenther in England.

In 1913 C. Tate Regan, then a young ichthyologist, and later the director of the British Museum, made a careful study of the whole group of viviparous killifish and discovered that the structure of the male's anal fin, or gonopodium, was a valuable index in finding relationships between members of this group of fish.

Regan came to the conclusion, after reading the previous publications in English, Spanish, German, and Italian, that the three fish mentioned above were really merely color varieties of a single species, and accordingly ruled that only one name should be used to represent it. In choosing the scientific name from the three given to it, Regan was bound by International Rules of Nomenclature. The code rules that the first name applied to a specimen must be preserved, provided it does not already refer to a different animal or group of animals.

The first name, *"Poecilia reticulata,"* of Peters (1859) was considered. But it so happened that there were many species of *Poecilia,* such as *vivipara, parae,* etc., and none of them bore generic relationship to *Poecilia reticulata* according to Regan's studies. The next generic name, proposed by Filippi, was then considered. Since *Lebistes* had never been used before, it was found suitable. The fish was therefore designated by Regan in 1913 as *"Lebistes reticulatus,"* the scientific name which it bears to this day. The change of *"reticulata"* to "reticulatus" was made on grounds of gender. Actually, then, the name changing of *"Girardinus guppii"* of old aquarists to *"Lebistes reticulatus"* of modern aquarists was the by-product of simplification. The service which Regan rendered deserves approval, although it did bring some temporary confusion to aquarists in 1913.

Think of the chaos which might have resulted if Regan had not pointed out the similarity of the fish referred to by three scientific names, each proposed in a different country. If an aquarist looking in a catalogue saw the names *"Poecilia reticulata,"* *"Lebistes poeciloides,"* *"Girardinus guppii,"* he might readily believe there were three different species of a special colorful Poeciliid fish from northern South America being offered for sale. He would be disappointed, to say the least, to find that what he really had bought were merely three varieties of the same fish species.

Applying different names to the same fish is a practice not restricted to the scientists. *Lebistes reticulatus* has traveled under the following common names in addition to the usual one of "Guppy": "Peacock Fish," because of the brilliant colors of the males; "Rainbow Fish," for the variety of colors in the males; "Millions Fish," for their great abundance and rapidity of reproduction and, finally, "Belly Fish," because the females are distended when gravid and heavy with young. The practice of giving names is simply the expression of man's tendency to describe things in his own personal way and frequently his dissatisfaction in accepting the names offered by others.

The Basic Categories

The word "variety" is often used by aquarists in the same sense that the word "species" is used here. The zoologist uses the word "varieties" to represent different color variations and other minor deviations within a population of animals of a single species. For instance, there are four species of fish in the genus *Xiphophorus*. These are: *Xiphophorus couchianus*, from Rio Grande; *Xiphophorus xiphidium*, from Rio Soto la Marina; *Xiphophorus variatus*, from Rio Panuco; and *Xiphophorus maculatus*, from Rio Papaloapan. Each species may have a number of varieties. The species *Xiphophorus maculatus* has many varieties, known to the aquarist as the Red, Black, Blue, Gold, Leopard, Crescent Moon, Twin-spot, One-spot, or Comet Platies, and many more, which include the newly developed Wagtail Platy. Varieties may be referred to by common names followed by their scientific name, as for example, Gold Platy (*Xiphophorus maculatus*). In general, different species of a genus come from different geographical localities. Varieties of species usually occur together in the same locality and freely interbreed.

To illustrate the zoological standing of a common aquarium fish, the following are the various divisions of the animal kingdom to which the Blue Platy belongs:

Kingdom—animal, Phylum—*Vertebrata*, Class—*Teleostomi*, Order—*Cyprinodontiformes*, Family—*Poeciliidae*, Genus—*Xiphophorus*, Species—*maculatus*, Variety—Blue Platy.

The more important groupings of some common aquarium fish are indicated in the following table:

EXAMPLES	GENUS AND SPECIES	FAMILY
Guppy	*Lebistes reticulatus*	*Poeciliidae*
Medaka	*Oryzias latipes*	*Cyprinodontidae*
Neon Tetra	*Paracheirodon innesi*	*Characidae*
Jack Dempsey	*Cichlasoma biocellatum*	*Cichlidae*
Fighting Fish	*Betta splendens*	*Anabantidae*
Zebra Fish	*Brachydanio rerio*	*Cyprinidae*

Each organism is given two names, a specific name (*reticulatus*) and a generic name (*Lebistes*). In scientific nomenclature, the more important name (corresponding to the family name of people) comes first, and that which corresponds to the Christian name comes second. Only the first scientific name is usually capitalized.

As indicated for the Platy, there may be many species in one genus. Whether or not a fish belongs to this or that genus, or is new to science, is determined by study of the structure of the body. In viviparous killifish, the details of structure of the male's anal fin provide a good indication of relationship. This fin passes through a remarkable metamorphosis. In the immature fish, it is flat and unbent, but as sexual development progresses, the male's anal fin becomes folded over itself, forming a trough. By means of this apparatus, and a powerful muscle to direct its action, the milt of the male passes to the female and thus internal fertilization is effected. The structure of the male's anal fin in viviparous fish is very complicated. Large series of these gonopodia from many fish are illustrated by Regan in his paper. The fins are quite remarkable, some are short, others are long; some have one hook, others have two hooks; some have long filaments and others have soft pouches. The functions of many of the peculiar structures within the gonopodium have yet to be discovered.

The four species of Platies have much the same type of gonopodal structure, consequently they are all classed under *Xiphophorus*. The Swordtail's anal fin is almost the same as the Platy's, but its tip has two hooks instead of one. Since there is a general similarity, both the Platy and the Swordtail are placed in the same genus, *Xiphophorus*. The Guppy (*Lebistes*) has a soft membranous hood, or prepuce, on its gonopodium. Curiously enough, *Mollienesia* also has a similar structure. Both are therefore included in the same tribe, *Poeciliini*.

Judging from the above, one might expect to hybridize the Platy and the Swordtail, and we know this is quite easily done. Also, one might have better luck in attempting to hybridize the Guppy and Mollie rather than in trying to mate the Guppy with the Platy or Swordtail. This is assuming that large structural and mechanical differences, as reflected in the structure of the intromittent organ, are important. In some cases, the visible differences are indeed the most important, but in others, the hidden differences in the microscopic cell details, as in chromosomes of the sex cells, are far more important.

Look at some of the aquarium advertisements and you will find them reading as follows: "We have one hundred *varieties* of tropicals in stock." What is really meant is species, not varieties. You often see: "We are specializing in the Platy family." There is not such group as the Platy *family*. Platies belong to the *technical family* of *Poeciliidae,* but so do Guppies, Mollies, and many more. It would be far better merely to say, "We are specializing in the Platies," or "in the Platy group," or "in the varieties of Platies."

Many aquarists write *"Lebistes Reticulatus," "Barbus Ticto,"* capitalizing both names as they would John Jones and Tom Smith. The first part is correct; *"Lebistes"* and *"Barbus"* are capitalized because they are *generic* names. But *"reticulatus"* and *"ticto"* are specific names, and they are written with a small letter; *Barbus ticto, Lebistes reticulatus.* If the specific name is the Latinized form of a man's name, is *may* be written with a capital as *Xiphophorus Hellerii* (Jacob Haekel coined that name in honor of Herr Heller, the Austrian horticulturist), but it is also correct to write it *Xiphophorus hellerii* (by the way, notice the two i's). The name of the author, first to describe the animal, has his name placed at the end of the italicized scientific name, as *Xiphophorus hellerii* Haekel.

Chapter 12
Aquarium Genetics
By Dr. Myron Gordon

Genetics, the study of heredity, is playing an increasingly important role in agriculture and medicine. Although aquarists may be aware of the benefits that have resulted from the application of genetic principles to the breeding of farm animals, they probably have not considered that the same principles could be applied to their domesticated fish. Moreover, they may not know that many scientific investigations have already been made on inheritance in fish and that these studies have made fundamental contributions to the science of genetics. Fish fanciers themselves have benefited, too. For example, the popular Black Wag Platyfish and Swordtail and the Bleeding-heart Platy all resulted from the deliberate use of well-established genetic techniques.

Mendelian Laws of
Inheritance in Aquarium Fish [1]

The best way to understand the working of Mendelian laws of inheritance is to conduct a simple experiment yourself. Before keeping tropical fish became nationally popular, mice, rats,

[1] Reprinted from *The Aquarium*, 2: 42–48; 50. June, 1933. Changes have been made to reflect currently correct nomenclature.

guinea pigs, and certain insects were universally used in these studies of heredity. Plants of many species were used, too; indeed, Mendel himself discovered the laws of inheritance by study of the common pea.

The tropical-fish keeper will be interested to know that some of his fish are excellent material for genetic work. Three species have been used with great success by geneticists (scientists who study inheritance phenomena), the Medaka (*Oryzias latipes*), the Guppy (*Lebistes reticulatus*), and the Platy (*Xiphophorus maculatus*).

The author's own work has been concerned with the Platyfish. Since the Platy is one of the most common of all tropical aquarium fish, and the characteristics studied are quite distinct and easily recognizable, this species will be used to illustrate how the laws of Mendel operate. The reader is urged to set up similar matings, for it is amazing how much interest can be aroused from a personal investigation of these remarkable laws of nature.

Several precautions are of paramount importance for accurate work with viviparous fish. The female fish that are to be used for studies of inheritance must never have been mated before, because a female fish that has once mated carries the sperms of the male in her body for as long as six months.

Both the males and females must come from pure breeding lines. For example, if you wish to cross a Gold Platy with a Gray Platy, the Gold Platy should come from a strain that produces Gold Platy offspring only. Similarly, the Gray Platy parent should come from a family of 100 per cent Gray Platy offspring.

Inheritance of Gray in the Platyfish

The simplest law of inheritance may be illustrated by mating a gray-colored Platy with a common Gold Platy. Owing to the fact that the plain gray-colored Platy is difficult to obtain from dealers because of its so-called uninteresting color pattern, the Blue Platy may be used; but pay no attention to the iridescent qualities or to the black blotch in front of the tail which may be present. These characteristics are also inherited, but success in the interpretation of the results of breeding experiments depends upon concentration of attention on *one* characteristic at a time. The restriction of study to *one* characteristic at a time was the key to success of Mendel over preceding plant and animal breeders. As experience is gained, two or more characteristics may be studied simultaneously.

The diagram below illustrates the mating of a Gray Platy father with a Gold Platy mother. These are the *parental* fish and are referred to as P_1. Many gold sisters of the Gold Platy mother may be crossed with gray brothers of the father in order to get a large number of offspring. Since the accuracy of interpretation of results of breeding depends upon the number of each type that appears, it is fundamental to get large broods. Where one mating will not provide sufficient young, many similar matings should be set up.

When a Gray Platy father is mated with a Gold Platy mother, it will be found that *all* the offspring will be Gray Platies. This means that the gray is *dominant* to gold. This, in turn, may be expressed as follows: gray (gold), where gold in the parentheses is represented but is temporarily suppressed by the presence of gray. Another way of expressing this same case is to let the capital letter S represent gray and the small letter s represent gold. The gray parent then is SS and the gold parent is ss, and their offspring become Ss. The offspring appear gray because S is *dominant* over s. The offspring, Ss, are indistinguishable from their father, SS.

The parental fish, it will be remembered, are referred to as P_1 and are symbolized as SS or ss. The fish resulting from this cross represent the first generation, or the first *filial* generation, and are referred to as F_1, and symbolized as Ss.

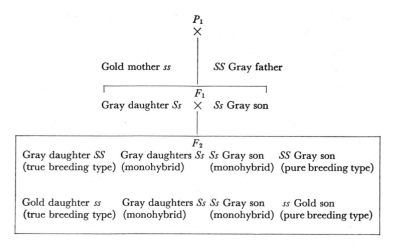

The first generation is represented by gray fish. It will be found that some of these fish will develop into males and others into females; the proportion of males to females will be approximately one to one.

If the first generation (F_1) gray females (Ss) are mated to their gray brothers (Ss), and if counts are kept as to the color of their offspring, it will be found that there will be approximately *three* gray fish to every *gold* one. These second-generation fish are referred to as F_2. If the F_2 fish are reared to sexual differentiation, it will be found that in the gray group 50 per cent of them are males and 50 per cent females. Similarly, in the gold group of the F_2 fish, the sex ratio, males to females, will be as one is to one.

How did the ratio of *three to one* (three gray to one gold) appear in the number of the second generation, and what does it mean?

Before answering these questions, let us repeat the same experiment from the beginning but merely reverse the colors of the (P_1) parents. In other words, instead of using a gray father and a gold mother, let us mate a pure gold father with a pure gray mother. This is called the *"reciprocal"* cross. In this case, the gold father may be represented by the symbols *ss* (small *ss*) and the gray mother by *SS* (large *SS*).

From the diagram on this page it will be seen that in this case *all* the offspring (F_1) are gray (*Ss*). When these grow up, it will be found that there are approximately as many males as females. When these F_1 *Ss* offspring are mated together and the offspring of the second generation are sorted, it will be discovered again that there are *three* gray fish to every gold *one*. Again, also, the sex ratios are one to one in each group. In other words, exactly the *same* results are obtained in the reciprocal cross as in the original one. This is of great significance.

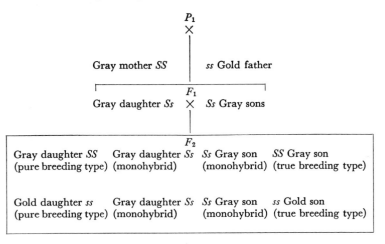

To answer the question as to the meaning of the *three to one* ratio and the significance of the similar results obtained in the original mating and its reciprocal, we must resort to the use of a few symbols and arrange them in a diagrammatic way to represent parent and offspring.

From the observations that direct and reciprocal crosses yield *similar* results, we may conclude that the offspring inherit equally from their paternal and maternal parents.

The symbols *SS* of the first cross indicate the hereditary constitution of the gray father and *ss* the hereditary constitution of the mother. The hereditary elements, the sperms of the males, each carry hereditary factor *S* in the single phase, and each egg of the mother carries the hereditary factor *s* in the single phase. At the time of mating, the *s* eggs become impregnated with *S* sperms—the fertilized egg *Ss* results, which hatches into a gray *Ss* fish. Similarly, in the reciprocal cross, the gray mother produces *S* eggs, and these are impregnated with *s* sperms; the result is an *Ss* offspring entirely similar to those produced in the original cross.

Now when brother and sister gray fish of the first generation are crossed, we may diagram the mating as follows:

$$Ss \left(\begin{matrix} \text{son} \\ \text{father} \end{matrix}\right) \times \left(\begin{matrix} \text{daughter} \\ \text{mother} \end{matrix}\right) Ss$$

The sperms of the father are of two kinds: *S* or *s*.

The eggs of the mother are of two kinds: *S* or *s*.

The sperm *S* may impregnate egg *S*, producing an *SS* individual which is *gray*.

The sperm *S* may impregnate egg *s*, producing an *Ss* individual which is also *gray*.

The sperm *s* may impregnate egg *S*, producing an *Ss* individual which is *gray*, again.

Finally, sperm *s* may impregnate egg *s*, producing an *ss* individual which is *gold* and occurs only once out of every four individuals.

The results may be summarized as follows:

P_1 father is gray, *SS* x mother is gold, *ss*. Fathers produce sperms of *S* constitution only. Mothers produce eggs of *s* constitution only.

F_1 sons are *Ss*, daughters are *Ss*. Sons produce sperms, *S* or *s*, daughters produce eggs, *S* or *s*.

F_2 table of all possible combinations is as follows:

	F_1 Sperm, *S*	F_1 Sperm, *s*
F_1 Egg, *S*	F_2 *SS*, gray fish	F_2 *Ss*, gray fish
F_1 Egg, *s*	F_2 *sS*, gray fish	F_2 *ss*, Gold Platy

Summarizing, there are *three* gray Platies, but one of them is *SS* and two of them are *Ss*.

There is *one* Gold Platy which is *ss*.

The *SS* type of gray can be distinguished from the *Ss* type, not by sight, but by a breeding test only. When an F_2 Gray Platy is mated to a Gold Platy and only gray fish are produced, we may conclude that the F_2 Gray Platy tested was pure; and its genetic formula may be written as *SS* and its offspring as *Ss*. When another F_2 Gray Platy is mated to a Gold Platy and two types of offspring result, namely, gray and golds, and these occur in equal numbers, then we must conclude that the F_2 gray parent was not pure and its genetic formula must have been *Ss* and its offspring were either *Ss* (gray) or *ss* (gold). By making this test, one can find out which are the *true breeding types*. After this preliminary testing, the pure breeding forms may be crossed to each other, and in this way *a true breeding line may be established.* The Gold Platy, being a recessive-type *ss*, is always pure. If Gold Platies are mated to Gold Platies, they cannot normally throw any other color. If they do, it is probably an exceptional sport or mutation.

In a genetic sense, the nontrue breeding type *Ss* is called a "hybrid," monohybrid, or "mongrel." The latter term has been dropped and "monohybrid" is used. The word "hybrid," here used, should not be confused with the word "hybrid" used in connection with results of crosses between different species, and, indeed, between different genera. In this case, we must say the Platy-Swordtail hybrid is a "generic hybrid" and the *Brachydanio rerio* by *Brachydanio analipunctatus* is a "species hybrid."

Inheritance of Black (Nigra) in the Platyfish

A different type of inheritance may be illustrated by mating the *Black* Platy with a *not-black* type of Platy. The not-black type may either be a Gold or Gray Platy. For simplicity, let us take the Gray Platy.

When a Black Platy father, P_1, is mated to a Gray mother, P_1, the first-generation offspring, F_1, will be all black like their black father. If these black sons are mated to their black sisters, it will be discovered that there will be *three* black fish in the F_2 (the second-generation) brood to *every nonblack* or gray fish.

Concerning the *three-to-one* ratio obtained in the second generation from the mating of *black* x *nonblack,* it seems that this is the same as is found in the *gray* x *nongray* cross previously discussed. But the difference lies in the sex ratios shown. In the *gray* x *nongray* cross, there were males and females among the nongray fish of the second generation. In the *black* x *nonblack* cross, there are *only females* in the *nonblack fish group.* To compensate for the unisexuality of the nonblack fish, there are two males to every female in the black group of the second generation. This brings the sex ratio back to one to one.

Now if the reciprocal mating with the black and nonblack varieties of Platies is made, namely, a *black mother* and a *nonblack father,* total dominance of the black pattern will *not* be exhibited in the brood of the first generation. If a black mother is mated with a gray father, one-half of the first generation will be black while the other half is nonblack. If the young are reared to sex recognition, it will be found that all the F_1 *black fish are males* and all the *nonblack fish are females.* In other words, the black pattern of the P_1 female parent has *"crisscrossed"* to her F_1 sons while the gray pattern of the P_1 father has crisscrossed to his daughters. This type of inheritance is known as *"sex-linked inheritance"* because a particular character is associated with a particular sex.

By mating an F_1 black son with its nonblack sister, also of the F_1 brood, an interesting brood appears. Again there are 50 per cent black offspring and 50 per cent nonblack offspring in F_2. In each group, however, both males and females appear in the black group and in the nonblack, or gray, group. This is, of course, different from the F_1, because in the F_1, males were black and females were nonblack.

In order to explain the results of inheritance of the black pattern in face of the different evidence for the inheritance of the gray pattern, we must resort to a modified form of diagram.

The *eggs* of the black female fish *are unlike* with respect to hereditary carriers of the black pattern. In other words, 50 per cent of the eggs elaborated by the black female carry the hereditary factor for black pattern and half of them do not. Those that do not carry the black-pattern factor are female-determining eggs while the other with the black-pattern factor are male-determining.

Suppose the two qualities of the black females are designated as Z and W, then the egg containing black-pattern factor may be written as Z_N (N for nigra or black pattern) and W_n may be used to designate the nonblack pattern and female-determining (small n for lack of nigra or black pattern).

Assume, also, that the sperms of the male Platyfish are Z only, and since the male used in this cross is nonblack (black female x nonblack male), his formula will be $Z_n Z_n$ (small n's for lack of black).

Let us indicate what happens when a $Z_n Z_n$ male mates with a $Z_N W_n$ female.

$$P_1 \text{ sperms, } Z_n$$

P_1 egg, Z_N F_1 male, $Z_N Z_n$ = black males
P_1 egg, W_n F_1 female, $W_n Z_n$ = nonblack females

When an F_1 $Z_N Z_n$ black son is mated with a $Z_n W_n$ nonblack daughter, the following recombinations are anticipated:

	F_1 sperm, Z_N	F_1 sperm, Z_n	
F_1 egg, Z_n	F_2 male, $Z_N Z_n$	F_2 male, $Z_n Z_n$	= black and nonblack males
F_1 egg, W_n	F_2 female, $W_n Z_N$	F_2 female, $W_n Z_n$	= black and nonblack females

From the knowledge of the mode of inheritance of the black pattern in the Platy, it is possible to predict the sex of the young fish with great accuracy when certain types of crosses, using this character, are made. For instance, if a black female is mated with a not-black male (Gold Platy), it is to be expected that those fish which show the black pattern in the brood will later differentiate into males, while those that do not develop the black pattern will be females. Similar characters are present in fowl, and poultry husbandrymen use this knowledge of hereditary laws to cull out surplus males from their chicks.

Problem Suggested for the Reader

Above a solution has been attempted to be given to the problem of inheritance of gray (a simple Mendelian character) and black (a sex-linked character) and it has been indicated how many fish of each type appear in the first and second generation for each character. In addition, the probable sex ratio of each group was indicated.

Suppose, now, that both black and gray characters were present in one parent and none in the other. With the information already at hand, one should be able to trace, in advance of making the actual cross, the inheritance of both characters at the same time and indicate the frequency with which both characters appear in the offspring, the frequency with which either black or gray appears singly, and the frequency with which no character appears, the Gold Platy. Furthermore, the sex ratio for each group may be calculated in advance. Try to figure the results of the following two matings to the first and second generations:

1. Gold Platy mother (not gray, not black) x gray-black father.

2. Black-gray mother x Gold Platy father (not gray, not black).

When you have finished your figuring, check your answer with the answer below.

Answer to Problem

When a Gold Platy mother (not gray, not black) is mated to a gray-black father Platy, the results in the first generation (F_1) are: sons and daughters are black and gray.

In the second generation, the following proportions are expected (F_2):

SONS	DAUGHTERS
6 black, gray	3 black, gray
2 black only	1 black only
	3 gray only
	1 gold (not gray, not black)

When a black-gray Platy mother is mated to a Gold Platy father (not black, not gray), the results in the first generation (F_1) are: sons are black and gray; daughters are gray only.

In the second generation, the following proportions are expected (F_2):

SONS	DAUGHTERS
3 black, gray	3 black, gray
1 black only	1 black only
3 gray only	3 gray only
1 gold	1 gold

Further Examples of How Fish Inherit [2]

The results of mating the Gold Platy to the Gray Platy have already been illustrated. In this article, examples will be given of what happens when other Platies are crossed with the Gold Platy. Those to be so discussed are: the One-spot Platy, the Twin-spot Platy, the Crescent Platy, and the Moon Platy.

If we study the inheritance of each pattern separately as indi-

[2] Reprinted from *Aquatic Life,* 18:209–214, February, 1935.

cated below, we see in each case the complete dominance of the pattern introduced. When the first-generation intervarietal hybrids are mated together, we get, in the second generation, three Platyfish with a pattern to every Gold Platy (with no pattern).

MATING	FIRST GENERATION	SECOND GENERATION
1. One-spot x Gold Platy	all One-spot	3 One-spot, 1 Gold
2. Twin-spot x Gold Platy	all Twin-spot	3 Twin-spot, 1 Gold
3. Crescent x Gold Platy	all Crescent	3 Crescent, 1 Gold
4. Moon x Gold Platy	all Moon	3 Moon, 1 Gold

When two Platyfish are mated, each having a singular pattern, the new Platyfish combines the patterns of both its parents. For instance:

1. One-spot x Twin-spot produces a *One-spot Twin-spot* Platy (it has three spots).

2. One-spot x Crescent produces a *One-spot Crescent* Platyfish.

3. One-spot x Moon produces a *One-spot Moon* Platyfish (*you have to look closely*).

4. Twin-spot x Crescent produces a *Twin-spot Crescent* Platyfish.

5. Twin-spot x Moon produces a *Twin-spot Moon* Platyfish.

6. Crescent x Moon produces the celestial *Crescent Moon* Platyfish.

Now let us see what happens when two Platyfish are mated, each of which has two patterns. The results are surprising. Let us follow through the results when the domino-patterned One-spot Twin-spot Platy is crossed with the celestial Crescent Moon Platy.

One-spot Twin-spot x Crescent Moon Platyfish

According to simple Mendelian principles we should expect to get sixteen different types because there are four heritable patterns involved:

PLATY PATTERNS EXPECTED	PATTERNS OBTAINED
1. One-spot Twin-spot Crescent Moon	none
2. One-spot Twin-spot Crescent	none
3. One-spot Twin-spot Moon	none
4. One-spot Twin-spot	none
5. One-spot Crescent Moon	none
6. One-spot Crescent	obtained, 25%
7. One-spot Moon	obtained, 25%
8. One-spot	none
9. Twin-spot Crescent Moon	none
10. Twin-spot Crescent	obtained, 25%
11. Twin-spot Moon	obtained, 25%
12. Twin-spot	none
13. Crescent Moon	none
14. Crescent	none
15. Moon	none
16. (Gold Platy)	none

We expected sixteen Platyfish types, but we got only four of them; furthermore, of those that we did get, none has the exact combination that their parents had!

This is all very strange, and if you ask why it is that you do not get any other patterns except these four given immediately above, the answer is that the hereditary patterns one-spot, twin-spot, crescent, and moon belong to a common hereditary series technically called *"multiple allelomorphic series"*! The matter can be explained no further here. (For a source of statistics and a photographic record of all the pattern combinations, see footnote.[3])

One more point might be mentioned. The kind of inheritance that is treated here (*multiple allelomorphism*) was unknown to Mendel, that great discoverer of the fundamental principles of heredity. Someone has said that nothing new in heredity has been found since Mendel. This is not true. The science of genetics has gone far since Mendel. Even before Mendel, breeders did pioneer work. This Mendel freely admits in his reports. No one

[3] Gordon, Myron, and Allan C. Fraser, "Pattern Genes in the Platyfish (Inheritance of naturally occurring color patterns in the Mexican platyfish, *Platypoecilus maculatus*)," *Journal of Heredity* 22: 169–185, 1931.

knows better than present-day workers the great contributions that Mendel has made. They honor Mendel and call him the "Father of Genetics." Mendel's theories are still fundamental. They have guided his disciples to make further progress and extend the original principles.

These varieties are common aquarium types. Cross them yourself and experience the thrill of testing a biological principle in your aquaria.

Discovery of the Gold Platyfish [4]

Any gold miner will tell you that when you are lucky enough to discover gold you do not usually find that noble metal in a pure state. Often the run-of-the-mine ore is pretty poor stuff, for gold in nature has many baser physical and chemical associates. Refiners through various technical processes isolate the pure metal, or combine gold with known quantities of other metals.

So with the Gold Platyfish. There are no *pure* Gold Platies in nature—or in the *rios* and *arroyos* of southern Mexico. Yet in every Platy in Mexico there is the making of a Gold Platy. It can further be said (and the chances of its being right are good) that if you have Platies in your aquarium, no matter what their superficial colors may be, and you may have the Red or Ruber, the Blue or Gray Platy, your Platies are in part Gold Platies. Most Platies are Gold Platies, basically; the gold color of the masquerading Platy is hidden by other pigment effects. Get rid of the reds and grays and black spots and you will have gold as a residue.

If, however, you have a White Platy or an Albino Platy, you do not have a Gold Platy, but you have something far rarer. You may refer to your true White Platy, quite appropriately, as the Platinum Platy.

When it was said, among other things, that the *Ruber* Platy is

[4] Reprinted from *The Journal of Heredity* (organ of the American Genetic Association), 26: 96–101, 1935.

a Gold Platy, plus a disguise, it was meant that the Ruber Platy is a Gold Platy plus a Red Platy plus a Black-spotted Platy plus a Gray Platy. In other words, the Ruber Platy is a composite of four distinct color varieties, each of which may be, and has been, isolated, or, to use a technological term in gold mining, "refined." The metallurgist's technique of purification is by means of chemical and physical analyses. The fish fancier's technique is selection, appropriate mating, and inbreeding.

If there are no *pure* Gold Platies in Mexico's streams, where did the first *pure* Gold Platy come from? From what strain of Platy was it isolated? After it was obtained, how was it multiplied to produce the pure race of true-breeding Gold Platies?

Let us review, hastily, a few suggestions on some of these points in four American aquarium encyclopedias. They say that the first true Gold Platy appeared ready-made as a sport, about fifteen years ago, in an aquarium of a German fish fancier. Upon this point there is inspiring accord, for witness these quotations:

Stoye—"The Gold Platy is a sport . . . a variation that occurs unexpected in nature."

Mann—"The Gold Platy is a sport . . . a freak of nature."

Uhlig—"The Gold Platy is a color mutation. . . . It just happened in the aquarium of a fancier who . . . appreciated it and 'fixed' it."

Peters—"A sport in nature is a sudden departure from the typical form of color. . . . The Gold Platy was such a sport. . . . Just what method was used in the propagation is not known."

As you see, they say that the Gold Platy is a sport but its genealogy is unknown.

The First Gold Platyfish

The first question: Where did the first Gold Platy appear?

Herr Otto Struve, a German fish fancier, produced it first in a pure form and named it, exactly fifteen years ago. In his paper published in 1920 he promised to tell us how he developed the Gold Platy, but, alas, nothing more was ever said. Herr Sachs tried to come to his rescue, two years later, and made many suggestions relying upon some experimental work on permanent color changes in other animals, but his ideas cannot be regarded as very plausible in the light of modern work in biology. While Herr Struve does not say how he got his Gold Platies, he drops a hint that turns out to be most significant. He says that a man had described a *golden* Platy, lightly spotted with black, in the *Wochenschrift* in 1916 and again in 1918. This clue is too good to be passed up. The description of these is found to have been written by Herr Friedr. Kammerzell; here is a brief abstract of the salient points of his very illuminating notes:

"A brown Platy female with black spotted sides [*braun mit schwarzer Seitenzeichnung*]" gave birth to some unusually marked and colored animals. The ground color of the new adult fish is *yellowish red and they are marked with black spots*. When young, the new Platies are pale yellow and fairly transparent; the black spots, which are to develop in a decided manner later, are barely visible. Since, to his knowledge, the female had been with no Platy male, Kammerzell thought these unusual golden young were the product of hybridization with some other species. Later he gives up the idea.

The brown, black-spotted female Platy which Kammerzell describes as the mother of the yellow brood is undoubtedly what we now know as the old-fashioned Ruber Platy, in which the males are brilliant red, but the females are dull red.

Kammerzell relates sadly his experiences with the golden, black-spotted Platies. He lost his original brood of golden Platies owing to the difficulties of getting fuel during the winter while the great war was going on. He was elated when another female, in 1918, produced a brood of *"twenty young among which I found five which showed that striking gold color."* Again these golden Platies are black-spotted. This ratio of *one* golden Ruber to *three* normal Rubers is the hereditary clue that will eventually solve the problem of the Gold Platy's origin. But no help in its solution comes from Herr Kammerzell directly. Herr Kammerzell whets our appetite for an explanation of these unusual Platy goings-on by saying that he plans "to show how a normally colored parent may produce young which in part exhibit totally dissimilar color." But, sad to relate, he, like Struve, fails to appear with the story.

Two important facts are gleaned from the reports of Kammerzell and Struve: the first *goldlike Platy* appeared in the Kammerzell Brothers' aquaria not later than 1916. The first *true Gold Platy* was reported by Herr Struve in 1920. The Kammerzell Gold Platies were black-spotted; Struve's Platies were *not* spotted. Are these phases of the Gold Platy (one spotted, the other nonspotted) related? If it can be shown that they are then this and one other link in the hereditary chain, when properly arranged, should solve the problem of the origin of the pure Gold Platies. One link will join the old-fashioned Ruber Platy to the golden Rubers of Kammerzell. The second link will join the golden Rubers to the pure Gold Platies of Struve.

The First Link: The Ruber to Golden Ruber

There seems to be no question about the fact that Kammerzell's golden Ruber Platies were derived from the old-fashioned Ruber, for even Kammerzell's 1918 paper is entitled: *"Ueber Gelbfärbung (Xanthorismus) bei Platypoecilus maculatus rote Varietät."* He says his *"rote Varietät"* is black-spotted.

How was it possible for Kammerzell to have obtained five golden Rubers in a brood of twenty? Some may suggest that these five golden Rubers were sports. But sports rarely, if ever, occur in 25 per cent of the brood. They are probably the first visible result of a sport to the Gold far back in their Ruber Platy family tree. It is as if we were witnessing a *première* performance of a play of the five golden Platies. We know that the golden Platies must have existed before in rehearsal, but they were hidden from our view and we did not see them until the opening night.

Because there were five golden Rubers to fifteen normal gray Rubers in the show under Kammerzell's tent, the hereditary spotlight (the three-to-one ratio) focuses attention on one of the *grandparents* of these five golden Rubers. These five golden Rubers are merely the actors making their initial bow. The author of the play goes back two generations. The golden actors owe everything to their grandfather Ruber who was given gold-developing qualities by a stroke of nature. Some call it "sporting," or "mutating," to the gold. Touched to gold by nature, this grandfather Ruber Platy was, nevertheless, unable to display its inheritance, for two gold elements are necessary before a Platy can be gold-colored.

This grandfather Ruber Platy passed on its potential gold-developing power to its offspring. Throughout the lifetime of these young, too, the display of gold was withheld from public view, for while one-half of the young Rubers inherited one gold-developing element from their father, none of them had the two gold elements necessary for the complete developments of a gold costume.

The *première* performance of the gold act, in the formal dress of gold, takes place when the second generation appears. One-fourth of the young have managed to collect two golden hereditary elements and have stepped forward into the public gaze for the first time in glittering costumes of gold. Those satisfied with superficialities would bestow glory on the first five golden Ruber actors, but those who know give the credit to their creator, their grandfather Ruber. Plain though he appeared, it was he who led his tribe along the golden path.

The origin of the golden Rubers may be told in a more matter-of-fact way. *A sport to the Gold occurred in a Ruber Platy, one of the grandparents of Kammerzell's golden Ruber Platies.* This mutation to the gold in the Ruber Platy affected one of the pair of hereditary color factors which governs the development of small black pigment cells that make the fish look gray. The effect of this mutation to the gold in the grandfather Ruber Platy was not revealed because the other and normal color factor of the gray-gold pair remained constant. The consequences of this mutation in the grandfather Ruber affected the Ruber's breeding performance but not its appearance. When mated to a normal Ruber, the Gold sport grandfather Ruber spread the new hereditary color factor, gold (lack of gray pigment cells) to many (just half) of its offspring, but at this point, his sons and daughters of the first generation were no different from the usual Ruber in appearance.

When, by pure chance, two gold-carrying Rubers of the first generation, each of which carries one gold factor, mate, there is opportunity for two gold factors (one from each parent) to combine, and a gold offspring is born in the second generation. As a matter of chance, if two such gold-carrying Rubers mate, there will be among their offspring *one* Gold Platy to every *three* normal ones. This briefly sets up a hypothetical case which gives us results similar to those reported by Kammerzell.

The Second Link: Golden Ruber to Gold Platy

How can we get a pure Gold Platy of the Struve type from the golden Rubers of Kammerzell? Wait for another sport? This is not necessary. Mate the golden, spotted Ruber of the Kammerzell type to a Gray Platy. The Gray Platy has *no* large black spots and *no* red body color. If a golden Ruber female is mated to a Gray male as stated, normal-looking Ruber males with spots and gray-looking females without spots appear. It looks as if the gold standard-bearers desert their colors. This is more apparent than real, for note what happens.

When the normal-looking gray daughters mate with their normal-looking Ruber brothers, quite an array of variously colored

Platies appears. Each type of Platy appears in a definite numerical ratio; among every three graylike Platies there is one goldlike Platy; and for every golden Ruber there is one pure Gold Platy. The color types of Platies line up in this manner:

FEMALES	MALES
3 Ruber (gray and spotted)	3 Ruber (gray and spotted)
1 golden Ruber (spotted)	1 golden Ruber (spotted)
3 gray	3 gray
1 pure gold	1 pure gold

By selecting the pure-gold females and males and mating them, it is easy to get a pure breeding line of Gold Platies. This part of the story is not a description of a theoretical setup; experiments similar to these have been performed time after time. No claim is made that Struve deliberately obtained his Gold Platies in the manner described. It is entirely possible that, by sheer chance, unbeknown to Struve, a series of matings such as outlined above led to the establishment of the pure-gold line.

Struve insists that his Gold Platies did not descend from Ruber Platies because *his Gold Platies throw only gold-colored young.* This is not good reasoning. His Gold Platies breed true because the Gold Platy is a recessive in inheritance. It hides nothing; it cannot produce anything else when mated to its own type.

Here, then, are the questions asked and their answers:

Q. Where did the first pure Gold Platy appear?

A. It appeared in the aquarium of Herr Otto Struve not later than 1920.

Q. What were the ancestors of the pure Gold Platy?

A. The old-fashioned Ruber produced the Kammerzell golden Ruber. The golden Ruber, when mated to a Gray Platy, produced the pure Gold Platies in the second generation.

Q. How was the pure Gold Platy strain established?

A. It was established by inbreeding the Gold Platies.

Black Lace for the Gold Platyfish [5]

This story begins in a small stream hidden in the hot, mite-infested jungles of Mexico's southern state of Oaxaca and stops, for the present, in the tanks behind the counters of any pet shop in New York.

According to reports from the recent tropical-fish exhibit held by the Aquarium Society of New York at the American Museum of Natural History, and from statements of sales from tropical-fish dealers all over the United States and Canada, the golden Wagtail Platyfish, an old favorite in a dazzling new costume, has climbed close to first place in the popular demand as a toy fish for the home aquarium. Yet only three years ago, one of the grandparents of these colorful, home-bred and reared aquarium fish was the wild, gray, undistinguished Platyfish that abound by the thousands in the arroyos and lagoons of the southern states of Mexico.

Within a few fish generations, by a system of careful selection and scientific breeding, the olive-drab body color of the wild Platyfish has been transformed to bright gold; and each fin of the wild specimens, which was colorless, has been darkened to produce the effect of an old-fashioned black-ribbed lace fan. The sharp contrast of dull black on bright gold in the new golden Wagtail Platyfish is particularly appealing, for rarely is this striking color scheme seen in fish.

The new Wagtail Platies are fine living examples of what cordial Pan-American cooperation may produce, for they are the direct result of mating a wild Mexican Platyfish with the domesticated Gold Platy which was perfected in the United States.

With the consent of the Mexican government and the generosity of the John Simon Guggenheim Memorial Foundation of

[5] Reprinted from *Animal Kingdom* (organ of the N.Y. Zoological Society), 46: 18–20, 1943.

New York, an expedition was organized with the cooperation of the New York Aquarium in 1939, for the purpose of studying the fresh-water fish of the Atlantic coastal rivers of Mexico. A book on this research is being prepared.

Large collections, particularly of the Platyfish, were made for special studies which have been going on for many years in connection with the problems of species origins and cancerous growths. Altogether, we collected more than eight thousand specimens, and when they were classified, we found some 135 different color types among them. This proves, we believe, that the southern Platyfish, *Xiphophorus maculatus,* is North America's most variable wild vertebrate with respect to color patterns. Yet in none of these patterns was there anything that remotely resembled the Wagtails of today. Among them was a variety which was distinguished from others by a black line on the upper and lower margin of the tail. The rest of the tail was transparent, as were all the other fins. We called this color type "the comet." A number of these, together with a larger assortment of other types of Platyfish, were shipped four thousand miles north to our Aquarium laboratories.

The Comet Platy, at the Aquarium, was subjected to a routine breeding test to see whether its pattern was inherited or whether it was just a chance variation that occasionally appears and then disappears without leaving any living representative to carry on the type. The test was simple. A wild Platy with the comet markings was mated with another Platy without them. We found that their offspring all had the comet pattern; and when these offspring were mated together, they produced three fish with the comet pattern to every plain type. This indicated to us, clearly, that the comet was inherited.

Then a Comet Platy of our original wild stock was mated to the Plain Gold Platy, a strain that has been domesticated for a long time, the first of which appeared twenty years ago. When their young were born, one could easily see that the gray body color of the wild Platy was dominant, for all the young were gray. Later, as the gray hybrids developed, their tails became darker and darker. And when they were about half an inch long, the other fins darkened, too. These were the first Black Wagtails, so named because of their wagging black tails.

Among our domesticated animals, the color scheme of the Siamese cat is comparable to that of the gray Wagtail Platyfish because its feet, tail, and snout are so much darker than its body; so are, to a lesser degree, the dilute fawn breed of the Great Dane dog and the Hampshire Down sheep. But above all others, the Himalayan rabbit and the giant panda, with their strong contrast of jet black extremities on a snow-white body, appealed to us as being the most attractive. So we used them as models in designing a somewhat similar costume for the Platyfish.

Since we already had the gray Wagtails, a plan to produce a black-finned and black-snouted Gold Platy was easily worked out. All we had to do was to mate the gray Wagtails to each other, or mate them back to the pure Gold Platy. We did both. In the first instance, we obtained the anticipated golden Wagtails once in about every seven young, or, to be exact, nine in every sixty-four. In the second case, we obtained the predicted and desired type once in every eight offspring. Later, when these black-finned Gold Platies were isolated and mated to each other, some bred true to type. Others produced a number of comets; these were throwbacks, indicating the Wagtail's ancestral origin, the wild comet-marked Platy.

The golden Wagtails have turned out to be so popular that fish breeders have used them to improve other varieties. Thus, now you can buy Red Platies with black fins; even the related Swordtail has been dressed up in black tails, gloves, and socks. But the golden Wagtail remains the key type and the most popular. Besides its sharply contrasting color scheme, there is another feature, the peculiar markings of its head, which enhances its attractiveness. The upper and lower margins of its jaws are outlined in black, and the black trim runs along the lower lines of its gill covers. It looks like a golden harlequin wearing a black mask. The golden Wagtail is an amusing fish to watch in the aquarium. It has the rare trick of exciting one's sense of humor. It is just the kind of fish that aquarists are looking for these days.

Back to Their Ancestors [6]

If a number of fancy breeds of an animal or of a plant be turned loose to mate at random, such a mixed population will tend to revert, in time, to its common ancestral type. Charles Darwin noticed this phenomenon in the free-living pigeons in the parks of London and described it in *The Variation of Animals and Plants under Domestication.*

Any person strolling in New York City's Battery Park, observing the variously colored pigeons that come fluttering down to pick up crumbs along the paths, may perceive this phenomenon of nature, for these wild flocks are under the control of no man. They appear to be a conglomerate stock, made up of escaped birds from the many lofts that rise above the tenements in lower Manhattan. A few pigeons are off-color, mottled black and white, or red and white; some are predominantly red, others deep blue, but the majority is like its ancestral type, the wild blue rock pigeon, *Columba livia.*

In the days before Gregor Johann Mendel, plant and animal breeders were puzzled by the appearance of "throwbacks" to the ancestral type. Now these are explained in terms of ordinary Mendelian inheritance. The reappearance of ancestral traits is usually brought about by the reunion of hereditary characters which had become separated during the period of their domestication.

[6] Reprinted from *The Journal of Heredity* (organ of the American Genetic Association), 32: 384–390, 1941.

Reversions in Plants and Animals

The plant breeder may obtain the original type of the sweet pea that is still found wild in Sicily by crossing the bush and cupid varieties; and by crossing two different white-flowering sweet-pea stocks the horticulturist may re-create plants having the wild purple flowers. The corn breeder, by mating two different stocks of dwarfs, can produce a plant normal in height. A rabbit fancier, by crossing the yellow rabbit with the Himalayan breed, may reestablish the wild agouti color.

According to Shisan C. Chen, the wild Goldfish (*Carassius auratus*) was first domesticated in China during the Sung Dynasty (A.D. 960–1278). Today Goldfish revert to their ancestral olive-green color so persistently that commercial breeders of the fancier color types find small pickings in any given brood. However, the case for reversion in the Goldfish is not complete, for many in a brood that are olive-green when young, if kept alive sufficiently long, eventually display the fancy colors of their breed.

Reversion at the Aquarium

A clear-cut example of complete color reversion in a tropical fish appeared at the New York Aquarium within the past year when a bright golden Swordtail was mated with an almost white, pink-eyed albino. The mating of these two light-colored domesticated Swordtail breeds produced the dark, olive-green, wild type, similar to those still found in the jungle streams of southern Mexico.

The wild Swordtails were imported into Europe for the first time in 1909, yet during this relatively short period of domestication a remarkably large number of color varieties were developed. The golden and the albino are but two out of a dozen or more strains.

The ancestral olive-green color is really a mosaic pattern of two kinds of tiny pigment-carrying cells, the blacks and the yellows. There are thousands of them in the skin of a Swordtail. For example, the area occupied by a single scale may have twenty black cells and almost as many yellow ones.

The Golden Swordtail

The Golden Swordtail owes its distinctive color pattern to the fact that it has lost all but a few black cells, but retains, in full force, all the yellow ones. It is like the quick-change artist in an old-time vaudeville show, who sheds one coat to reveal a more brilliant one beneath.

This change from the wild to the golden, from a full complement of many tiny black pigment cells to a rare few, may be expressed this way: The hereditary factor *St* representing the *stippling* effect of the small black cells in the normal wild Swordtail mutated from *St* to *st,* from the dominant phase to the recessive, from the olive-green phase to the golden. This must have taken place prior to 1921 for, in that year, Krasper, an aquarist, first described the golden sport. Later, another aquarist, Hildebrand, pointed out that, in one mating, the wild Swordtail was dominant over the golden. In 1934, the author showed, in a series of genetic tests, that the golden character in the Swordtaid was definitely recessive and was typically Mendelian. This has since been confirmed by Kosswig.

The golden sport indicates a breakdown in the Swordtail's ability to produce black pigment cells at a normal rate. What this failure is we do not know for certain. We do know that the machinery for black-pigment formation does not break down completely because the Golden Swordtail has black eyes and a few black cells along its black, but these are so few that they do not diminish its vivid yellow color. It may be that the Golden Swordtail fails to produce sufficient raw material in the color cells for normal pigmentation to develop. It may also be that the chemical constitution of the cell is different, so that the melanin reactions are not carried to completion.

Pink-eyed Albinos

The albino, with its white body and pink eyes, appeared suddenly about 1934. A few of them were discovered in aquaria containing the ordinary, black-eyed, olive-green Swordtails. Curiously, these mutants appeared almost simultaneously in American and in European aquaria. Once the albinos were detected and isolated, they were easily perpetuated by inbreeding. Like albinism in other animals, this character is usually recessive. Critical studies proving this were made by Kosswig and they have been confirmed by the author's experiments.

The albino mutation brought about the almost complete elimination of the black pigment cells normally present in the skin, in the retina of the eyes, and in many other areas of the body. The albino's eyes appear pink in the Swordtail not because of any special red pigment, but because, as in the pink-eyed albino amphibians, birds, and mammals, the clear lens of the eye transmits the color of the blood as seen through the many transparent blood vessels in the retina. The albino mutation involved a second hereditary factor influencing black pigment. In this instance, a dominant factor I representing the wild type mutated to the recessive i phase. The factor i stops practically all the machinery responsible for the production of black pigment. With the i factor in control, there may be an abundance of raw material for black-pigment production provided by the hereditary factor St, but none can be converted.

Wild Equals Golden Plus Albino

When a Golden Swordtail is mated with an Albino, the wild, fully pigmented Swordtail is re-created because each variety brings to its offspring the essential dominant factor which the other lacks.

From their golden parent, the wild, olive-green Swordtail offspring inherit the machinery (I), and from the Albino Swordtail they obtain plenty of raw materials (St) for the normal, large-scale production of black pigment cells.

This may be expressed in a diagram:

$$\text{Golden} \times \text{Albino} = \text{Wild, Olive-Green}$$
$$\textit{stst II} \quad \times \textit{StSt ii} \quad = \quad \textit{Stst Ii}$$

The wild-colored offspring of the Golden and Albino parents, after being mated brother to sister, are producing, out of every sixteen born, nine young that are typically wild, three that are Golden, and four that are Albinos. One of every four Albinos must be a double recessive, but as yet they cannot be distinguished from the ordinary Albinos. They may eventually turn out to be a more attractive variety; perhaps a superblond Swordtail will emerge.

Use for the New Albinos

Whether or not the new Albinos will be attractive is not particularly important. But they will be extremely useful in current genetic studies of melanomas that develop in fish hybrids when the Albino Swordtail and the Spotted or Black-banded Platyfish are mated. Breider and Kosswig have shown that when a Black-banded hybrid is back-crossed to an Albino Swordtail, and their Black offspring are back-crossed again to the Albino, some of the young of the last mating develop tumors without black pigment. With the cooperation of Fred Flathman of Woodhaven, Long Island, we have succeeded in obtaining fish hybrids with black tumors in the first generation and colorless tumors in the offspring of the second generation. Melanomas that are white instead of black are biological anomalies.

The ordinary Albino Swordtails transmit micromelanophores (the technical name of the small black pigment cells) to their hybrids, just as they transmit these same cells to their own wild, olive-green-colored young of their own species. With the development of the new strain of double-recessive Albinos, it will be possible to eliminate the micromelanophores which are regarded as nonessential for tumor production; thus, pathologically, the study of the colorless melanomas can be simplified. More emphasis will be placed upon the large black pigment cells, the macromelanophores, brought to the hybrid by the spotted Platyfish. Under the influence of the Albino factor, i, it appears that macromelanophores, just as the micromelanophores, cannot elaborate melanin pigment, yet the large colorless pigment cells may still be able to evoke colorless melanomas in the fish hybrids.

Practically nothing is known about the inheritance of melanomas in man, the mouse, or the horse; still less is known about human colorless melanomas. Melanoma studies with fish should be of value in interpreting the development of these neoplastic diseases in the more specialized vertebrates, including man. Specific proof of the closeness of fish to man with reference to the similarity of cell types in each has recently been indicated by Grand, Gordon, and Cameron, in a cooperative study between the New York Aquarium and New York University.

In the tissue-culture laboratory of the Department of Biology of the Washington Square College, the biologists were successful in growing, for the first time, tiny fragments of fish melanomas in a medium composed of fish serum and chick-embryo extract. They compared the cell types that emerged from the fish-melanoma fragment with the cells that emerged from fragments of mouse and human melanoma previously studied. They found that the cell types, the melanoblasts, the melanin-bearing macrophages, and the fibrocytes, in fish, in mice, and in men were identical in structure.

Conclusions

The mating of the Golden Swordtail with the Albino was conducted as a routine study of inheritance in fish, a subject of
which comparatively little is known. Reversion to the ancestral
color pattern was demonstrated. The double-recessive Albinos
obtained as a by-product of this study will be of great value in
explaining the curious pathological anomaly, colorless melanomas.

Chapter 13

The Balanced Aquarium Myth

By James W. Atz

The idea that the animals and plants of an aquarium balance each other in their production and consumption of carbon dioxide and oxygen was a little over one hundred years old when it was proven wrong. Although it was disproved nearly twenty years ago, the myth of the balanced aquarium still holds sway—in the tropical fish fancy, in the schoolroom, and in the laboratory. Such is the power of the too felicitous phrase, the too trim theory.

Joseph Priestley was the first to demonstrate the reciprocal action of plants and animals on the atmosphere, when he showed that a limited amount of air in which rats were smothered would again support more of them after green plants had remained in it for a time. In 1777 he also reported that fish affect the water in which they live in the same way that terrestrial animals affect the air surrounding them, although he apparently had not availed himself of Robert Boyle's experiments, performed a century earlier. In 1670 Boyle showed that a fish breathes air dissolved in water, since it dies when its container is placed in a chamber from which most of the air is exhausted by a vacuum pump or when its glass, "quite filled with water," is "so closely stoppered" that it "cannot enjoy the benefit of air."

Priestley paved the way for the fundamental work of Ingen-

[1] Reprinted from *The Aquarist and Pondkeeper*, 14: 159–160; 179–182, 1949. The original version appeared in *Natural History*, 58: 72–77; 96, 1949.

housz, de Saussure, and Senebier on plant physiology and of Lavoisier on the chemistry of animal respiration. Thus, by the first decade of the nineteenth century it was well established that plants, like animals, respire, taking in oxygen and giving off carbon dioxide, but that in the presence of strong enough light this function is far overbalanced by the assimilative one, later called "photosynthesis," in which carbon dioxide and water are consumed and oxygen released.

It is believed today that almost all the oxygen in our atmosphere results from the photosynthesis of plants, so the savants of Priestley's time were not incorrect in emphasizing the far-reaching importance of this plant-animal relationship. But they gave to it a teleological twist, using it to illustrate the marvelous goodness of the world in which man lives. Sir John Pringle, President of the Royal Society in 1773, declared:

From these discoveries we are assured that no vegetable grows in vain, but that from the oak of the forest to the grass of the field, every individual plant is serviceable to mankind; if not always distinguished by some private virtue, yet making a part of the whole which cleanses and purifies our atmosphere. In this the fragrant rose and deadly nightshade cooperate: nor is the herbage, nor the woods that flourish in the most remote and unpeopled regions unprofitable to us, nor we to them; considering how constantly the winds convey to them our vitiated air, for our relief, and for their nourishment.

This florid vein continued on into the cynical twentieth century, when J. E. Taylor wrote, in 1901, that

every teacher in physical geography now imparts to his class that the oxygen generated in the virgin forests of the Amazon valley may be brought by the wind to bring health to the fetid streets and alleys of crowded European cities, and that in return the carbonic acid breathed forth from our overpopulated towns may be carried on the "wings of the wind," to be eventually absorbed by the incalculable stomata which crowd the under surfaces of the leaves in the same forest-clad region!

These were the compost mixers for our myth; they prepared each successive generation with successively more fertile minds for its seeding and growth. Who, preoccupied with the worldwide implications of the balance between plants and animals, could suspect that so insignificant a part of the earth as a home aquarium would not conform?

The first aquarium: where and when was it devised? The word itself was not used to indicate a container of water with aquatic animals living in it until 1852; but before that, who was the first to keep fishes captive in some small, water-containing receptacle? As far back as 2500 B.C., the Sumerians kept living fish for food. The ancient Romans had pet Moray Eels and Mullet, while the Chinese domesticated the Carp more than two thousand years ago and the Goldfish in their Sung Dynasty (960–1278), but all these fish were maintained in pools or ponds. There is evidence, however, that in some places in China Goldfish were kept indoors in porcelain vessels during the winter months. Perhaps these were the first aquaria, although we cannot be sure.

If we consider the aquarium properly to be only a glass or glass-sided water container, we can fix its origins a little more definitely. The earliest record of putting fish into glass containers comes down to us from the Romans of the first century. They did not do this to keep the fish alive, however, but to watch their change of color as they died.

The maintenance of fish in small glasses was still noteworthy enough in 1746 to warrant the publication of Fellow William Arderon's letter on the "keeping of small fish in glass jars" in the *Philosophical Transactions* of the Royal Society of London; yet this was certainly not the first attempt to do so. According to Boyle, Guillaume Rondelet, a Renaissance student of aquatic life who died in 1566, once claimed that his wife had kept a fish alive in a glass of water for three years. Samuel Pepys, indefatigable recorder of minutiae, made the following entry in his diary on May 28, 1665: "Thence home and to see my Lady Pen, where my wife and I were shown a fine rarity: of fishes kept in a glass of water, that will live so for ever; and finely marked they are, being foreign."

But the keeping of fish as pets did not become a popular pastime until after the Goldfish was widely introduced into England during the first half of the eighteenth century. At first they were maintained in ponds on the lands of the well-to-do. Sir John Hawkins, noted editor of Izaak Walton and Charles Cotton, wrote in 1760: "There has also been lately brought hither from *China,* those beautiful creatures Gold and Silver Fish. . . . These fish are usually kept in ponds, basins and small reservoirs of water, to which they are a delightful ornament; and I have known a few of them kept for years in a large glass vessel like a punch-bowl. . . ." In the second and third editions of *The Compleat Angler* which he edited, dated 1766 and 1775 respectively, the above footnote was repeated, but in the fourth edition, printed in 1784, Hawkins saw fit to alter it, stating that "it is now a very common practice to keep them in a large glass vessel like a punch-bowl. . . . " The Reverend Gilbert White corroborates Hawkins in Letter LIV of *The Natural History of Selborne,* based on an entry from his Journal dated October 27, 1782: "When I happen to visit a family where gold and silver fishes are kept in a glass bowl, I am always pleased with the occurrence, because it offers me an opportunity of observing the activities and propensies of those beings with whom we can be little acquainted in their natural state."

If we accept this evidence at face value, we can declare that between 1775 and 1784 the Goldfish bowl became a popular household appliance in England.

The elements of our myth were now at hand; it only remained for someone to apply the principle of plant-animal balance to an aquarium by growing aquatic plants in it.

Looking at the matter in historical perspective, one is not impressed by the ingenuity of the idea or surprised that a number of people claimed to have stumbled upon it independently and more or less at the same time. The wonder is, perhaps, why no one hit upon it before. For it was not until after 1840 that aquarists began to employ aquatic plants in their tanks. Moreover, it was a French invertebrate zoologist, Charles des Moulins, who first claimed to have discovered that the presence of green plants in small containers of water kept that medium suitable indefinitely for small animals (planarians in this instance) and who attributed this effect to the physiology of the plants. Charles des Moulins was President of the Linnaean Society of Bordeaux, and he reported his experiments in the *Actes* of that organization in 1830.

Credit for the earliest clear enunciation of the benefits resulting from the interactions between aquatic plants and fish should, however, go to the author of the chemistry textbook, William Thomas Brande. As early as 1821, his *Manual of Chemistry* stated: "Fishes breathe the air which is dissolved in water; they therefore soon deprive it of its oxygen, the place of which is supplied by carbonic acid; this is in many instances decomposed by aquatic vegetables, which restore oxygen and absorb the carbon; hence the advantage of cultivating growing vegetables in artificial fish-ponds." That this information should appear in a book on chemistry makes one wonder if it were not common knowledge among fish culturists of the time, but a search of the literature has failed to reveal even an allusion to it.

Perhaps this disjunction of knowledge explains why the five or six amateur and professional biologists who at this time came upon the idea of using plants to "purify" their aquaria, each claimed to be the originator of it and why they quarreled (albeit genteelly) as to who was the first among them to do so.

One of them, Robert Warington, later said that it was Brande's statement that had incited him to set up his experimental tank with Goldfish and tape grass (Vallisneria). Warington was a chemist himself, and his was the first unequivocal exposition of the conception of mutual interdependence of the plants and animals in a small container of water. Both des Moulins and George Johnston, who had worked with sea water, marine animals, and seaweed previous to 1842, had been somewhat vague in their writings. Not so Warington. His paper, read before the Chemical Society of London early in 1850, is perfectly clear and could be used today as a summation of what practically all teachers, most aquarists, and many professional biologists believe:

Thus we have that admirable balance sustained between the animal and vegetable kingdoms, and that in a liquid element. The fish, in its respiration, consumes the oxygen held in solution by the water as atmospheric air; furnishes carbonic acid; feeds on the insects and young snails; and excretes material well adapted as a rich food to the plant and well fitted for its luxuriant growth.

The plant, by its respiration, consumes the carbonic acid produced by the fish, appropriating the carbon to the construction of its tissues and fibre, and liberates the oxygen in its gaseous state to sustain the healthy functions of the animal life, at the same time it feeds on the rejected matter which has fulfilled its purposes in the nourishment of the fish. . . .

The key word was "balance," and it appears in the writings of N. B. Ward, Philip Henry Gosse, Edwin Lankester, and Mrs. Anne Thynne, coclaimants for the honor of first applying the oxygen-carbon dioxide interactions of plants and animals to small aquaria. Probably the first to set up a tank containing both fish and plants with the idea of balancing one against the other was Nathaniel Bagshaw Ward, an English botanist, who originated the Wardian Case, that glass-sided box with ferns and other plants growing inside it so often seen in latter nineteenth-century parlors. Whether it was this miniature greenhouse (admittedly not airtight) that gave Ward the idea for setting up his aquarium in

1842 was never made clear, either by him or his encomiastical son. At any rate, the father did not publish an account of his work until 1852. Ward was apparently indirectly responsible for the first public aquarium. His tank inspired a Mr. Bowerbank to set up one of his own, and this in turn gave David W. Mitchell, Secretary of the Zoological Society of London, the idea of an exhibit made up of a series of such tanks. This took form in Regent's Park as the Fish House, which was opened to the public in the spring of 1853 and consisted of a number of standing aquaria, some with fresh, some with salt water, housed in a conservatory-like building.

Judging from the remarks of the times, the exhibition was a tremendous success. Moreover, it stimulated the hobby of keeping fish as pets at home so much that the maintenance of small aquaria became more or less of a craze. Dealers in tanks and aquatic plants and animals established themselves in London and Edinburgh. Prices for a readymade home aquarium ranged from two shillings to ten pounds. The experience of one J. Paul was perhaps typical: "I saw the aquarium first at the Regent's Park Gardens," he wrote, "then in a shop-window in the City Road, and then—everywhere; and I at once determined to be the happy possessor of a tank. Alas," he continued, somewhat ruefully, "I knew not the penalty attendant on this worship of Neptune."

Punch poked fun at the fancy in its issue of December 13, 1856:

> Oh, come with me,
> And you shall see
> My beautiful Aquarium;
> Or if that word
> You call absurd,
> We'll say instead Vivarium.
>
> 'Tis a glass case,
> In fluid space,

Where, over pebbles weedy,
Small fishes play:
Now do not say
You think they must be seedy . . .

My Dicky sings,
And claps his wings,
I know that what he wishes
Is to escape
His cage, and scrape
Acquaintance with the fishes.

Now tell me, do,
Suppose that you
Your mode of life could vary;
Which would you like?
To be my Pike?
Or to be my Canary?

By 1858, at least nine books on the keeping of home aquaria had been published in London, and an encyclopedia of 1854 included an article on the subject. In all these and in various newspaper and magazine articles, too, the idea of balance between the aquarium's plants and animals was stressed. Our myth was now firmly fixed in the common knowledge; a host of amateur aquarists practiced its precepts daily, and they and their friends saw living proof of it each time they looked into a tank.

There was living disproof of it to be seen also, but this was either overlooked or reasoned away. For many years previous, fish had been successfully maintained in bowls and tanks without any plant life in their water. How did that fit into the scheme? In 1856, Shirley Hibberd expressed the view taken by aquarists on this matter:

The Philosophy of the Aquarium must be clearly understood. . . . It is a self-supporting, self-renovating collection, in which the various influences of animal and vegetable life balance each other and maintain within the vessel a correspondence of action which preserves the whole. A mere globe of fish is not an aquarium in the sense here indicated; because to preserve the fish for any length of time, the water must be frequently changed. . . .

And yet hundreds of aquarists before and since have kept fish in tanks without plants and without changing the water for months on end. Hibberd himself kept a tank of Goldfish with no plants and without changing the water for seven years. He explained this by attributing the oxygenation of the water to microscopic and algal growths. He wrote that, although it may take some time for a tank

to become richly clothed with suitable oxygen makers, some supply of oxygen is secured from the very first, for I have seen ciliated spores and beginnings of genuine vegetable deposits within a few hours of the first furnishing of a tank. Hence it was that . . . I did not hesitate to introduce the fishes as soon as the tank was furnished, without waiting for the full development of the microscopic forest, for I knew that before the fishes exhausted the oxygen in the fresh river water, there would be the beginning of a new supply for them, and there was never any distress through that procedure.

Since fish can live in a newly set-up tank without any apparent plants at all—either introduced or grown *in situ*—there must be enough unseen ones present to oxygenate the water, else the fish would die! The reasoning was fallacious, but somehow the facts had to be made to fit the belief.

Conclusive proof of the falsity of Hibberd's assertions was given when it was shown that fish could live as long as four months under axenic conditions, that is, in vessels and water not only free of all higher plants and algae but absolutely free of all demonstrable bacteria and other microorganisms.

In addition, it has always been well known that at night or on dull days plants consume oxygen and give off carbon dioxide just as animals do. How did fish survive such periods in an aquarium? Was it by breathing oxygen that had been stored up in the water while the plants were producing it? No aquarist ever said so, but this was implied in some of their works. A little thought on the properties of oxygen dissolved in water would have shown this to be impossible. Some concepts are simply too good to discard, even if they are untrue; the balanced aquarium is one of them.

Proof that the balanced aquarium existed only in the minds of its devotees and an uncritical public was published in *Copeia* in 1931 by Charles M. Breder, Jr., at that time Research Associate at the old New York Aquarium in Battery Park. His proof that "the production of oxygen by the photosynthesis of plants in open balanced aquaria contributes little, if any, to that consumed by the animal life therein" was obtained most directly—simply by *measuring* the amount of oxygen present under different conditions. No one had ever bothered to do this before, and Breder found that as far as oxygen was concerned, an "over or under saturation returns with extreme rapidity to equilibria" with the air above the water. In other words, the water is practically never under or oversaturated with dissolved oxygen. As soon as the slightest deficiency in oxygen exists in a tank, oxygen from the atmosphere passes into solution to make it up. Similarly, if an excess is produced by plants under the influence of bright light, this quickly passes off into the air.

In fact, one might say: Just try to keep oxygen out! Research workers in fish physiology sometimes want to determine exactly how much oxygen a fish consumes, and to do this, they must measure the oxygen in a *sealed* container of water before and after a fish has lived in it. The problem is to get a seal that will keep out the atmospheric oxygen during the course of the experiment. Even $1\frac{1}{2}$ inches of heavy mineral oil, floated on the top of an aquarium's water, will not entirely keep out atmospheric oxygen from above, when the fish begin to use up the gas already dissolved in the water below. Scientists have had to design some complicated apparatus to circumvent this difficulty.

Despite this omnipresence of oxygen, every aquarist has at one time or another seen his fish gather at the surface of their tank, "gaping." What makes them come to the top, breathing rapidly, seeming to be in some sort of respiratory distress? Not a lack of oxygen, but an excess of carbon dioxide. Compared with oxygen, this gas passes from the water into the air and from the atmosphere into solution much more sluggishly. Consequently, when an excess amount of it appears in an aquarium, it takes an appreciable length of time for it to pass off. On the other hand, Dr. Breder found that in tanks where plants were actively engaged in photosynthesis—building up carbohydrates out of water and carbon dioxide and giving off oxygen—the carbon dioxide remained far below its equilibrium level with the atmosphere for extended periods.

Plants, then, can and do make an aquarium more habitable for aquatic animals by using up the carbon dioxide that the latter produce—carbon dioxide which, as Dr. Breder put it, is "the limiting factor as regards the respiratory gases." If plants were at work all the time, a tank containing them could support more animals than one without. But at night or on dark days, when they cannot carry on photosynthesis, plants breathe like animals, adding their share of suffocating carbon dioxide to the water. They breathe, of course, in bright light, too, but then their respiration is far outweighed by their photosynthetic activity, and they consume far more carbon dioxide than they produce. Without bright light, however, the presence of plants in a tank theoretically lessens the number of fish that that tank will support. Contrary to general belief, putting plants into an aquarium does not make it possible to keep more fish in it without suffocation taking place.

It has long been known that carbon dioxide in excess can kill fish or man. Both amateur and professional ichthyologists, however, have usually neglected the effects of this gas, assuming that oxygen alone was concerned with the respiration of fish. Whether or not a fish will be asphyxiated depends on the concentrations of both oxygen and carbon dioxide dissolved in the water. The more carbon dioxide present, the greater must be the concentration of oxygen to prevent asphyxiation. The principal reason for this seems to be that small amounts of carbon dioxide increase the efficiency with which the blood of a number of fish can deliver life-sustaining oxygen to the tissues but at the same time sharply decrease the ability of the blood to take on oxygen at the gills. Physiologists call this an "exaggerated Bohr effect."

The extent to which this effect operates in fish varies greatly from species to species. Trout, several Characins, and a number of marine fish have been demonstrated to be quite sensitive to carbon dioxide. Carp, Goldfish, and various armored Catfish show less sensitivity, and the common Bullhead shows hardly any at all. As would be expected, those species known by aquarists and fish culturists to be most easily asphyxiated are the ones whose blood is most affected by carbon dioxide.

It is possible for a fish to be unable to utilize oxygen that is present in ordinarily ample quantities all about it simply because there is too much carbon dioxide present. This must be the physiological explanation why carbon dioxide, and not oxygen, is the critical respiratory gas in an aquarium. As Dr. Breder discovered, there is always sufficient oxygen present, but carbon dioxide may build up to relatively high concentrations, since it is a slow-moving gas and can be produced by the respiration of the tank's inhabitants at a faster rate than it can escape through the water surface. The fish will then be starved for oxygen even though there is plenty of it around, because they cannot utilize it in the presence of excessive amounts of carbon dioxide.

The reason the aquarist gets along so well, even while working under the wrong premise, is that he is doing the right thing—for the wrong reason. For example, when he aerates his tank's water or circulates it, he is not introducing more oxygen, as he usually believes, but facilitating the escape of carbon dioxide.

"A vessel of water containing plants and animals must be

looked upon as a little world," wrote Edwin Lankester in 1856. We can now just as categorically state that it must *not* be so considered. Although the physiology of plants and animals in an aquarium is identical with the physiology of those in the world at large, the part they play in the ecology, or bionomics, of their tank is quite different from that taken by the sum total of all life in the earth's grand economy. In this sense, an aquarium is not at all a microcosm but merely a part of a macrocosm—part of a larger world from which it cannot be either physically or ideally separated. No balance could be expected to exist in such an open system. Looked at logically, the idea of a balanced aquarium, as far as respiratory gases are concerned, seems baseless. But then, most myths never made a pretense of being logical.

Does the balanced aquarium exist in any sense whatsoever? Most certainly, so far as the chemistry of the water is concerned. In a well-established fresh-water standing aquarium the water remains crystal clear and in a relatively static chemical state. This stability, or balance, can be most clearly brought out by comparing marine and fresh-water aquaria. Sea water, in which animals are living, continuously deteriorates in its ability to support life. That is the principal reason marine aquaria are so much more difficult to maintain than fresh-water ones.

Appendix

POPULAR NAME	SCIENTIFIC NAME	SOURCE	REPRODUCTION TYPE
Rasbora	*Rasbora heteromorpha*	Sumatra	Egg Layer
Catfish	*Corydoras paleatus*	So. America	Egg Layer
White Cloud Mountain Fish	*Tanichthys albonubes*	China	Egg Layer
Black Tetra	*Gymnocorymbus ternetzi*	Paraguay	Egg Layer
Blue Molly or Sphenops	*Mollienesia sphenops*	Bred in U.S.	Live Bearer
Albino	*All* the albino species in most fish, such as Paradise, Molly, and Guppy albinos, are light pink, with pink eyes. They are fairly difficult to breed successfully. They are more delicate than the normal fish. Their breeding habits are nearly always the same as those of the normal species to which they belong, except they require better care.		
Head and Tail Light	*Hemigrammus ocellifer*	Amazon River, So. America	Egg Layer
Featherfin	*Hemigrammus unilineatus*	S. America	Egg Layer
Jewel Fish	*Hemichromis bimaculatus*	Africa	Egg Layer
Angel Fish	*Pterophyllum scalare* and *P. eimekei*	Amazon River, So. America	Egg Layer

AQUARIUM TEMP.	DISPOSITION	FACTS ON BREEDING
70–90	peaceful	Female swims upside down against plants ejecting her eggs. Most eggs are lost. Remove parents after spawning. Eggs hatch 48 hours. Mature in 9 months.
70–85	very peaceful	Many eggs are carried by female on ventral fins to a selected spot in tank. Fry hatch 7–10 days. Leave parents.
70–85	peaceful	Drop nonadhesive eggs. Fry appear 48–72 hours. Remove parents after spawning.
70–90	very peaceful	Stock tank with quantity of Cabomba or other fine floating plants, also make vegetation thick on bottom. Eggs are semiadhesive and are deposited on plants. Remove parents after spawning. Fry hatch in 72 hours.
60–80	very peaceful	Easy to breed. Just place male and female together. Provide much vegetation. Parents usually disregard live young.
70–80	peaceful	Drop adhesive eggs on fine plants. More males are necessary than females. Fry hatch in 48 hours. Mature at 8 months.
70–80	peaceful	Spawns on fine plants. Adhesive eggs. Remove parents after spawning.
75–90	wild	Eggs are deposited on stones to which they stick. One parent incubates the eggs; after eggs hatch the fry are dependent on parents for first three days.
75–90	peaceful, but very timid	Hard to breed. Deposit adhesive eggs on smooth surface of aquarium or on Sagittaria. Eggs are incubated. Fry hatch in 8 days. A year is needed for maturity.

POPULAR NAME	SCIENTIFIC NAME	SOURCE	REPRODUCTION TYPE
Sparrman's Cichlid	*Tilapia sparrmani*	Southern Africa	Egg Layer
Mouthbreeder	*Haplochromis multicolor*	Egypt	Egg Layer
Orange Chromide	*Etroplus maculatus*	India	Egg Layer
Three-spot Gourami	*Trichogaster trichopterus*	India	Bubble-nest Builder
Blue Gourami	*Trichogaster sumatranus*	Sumatra	Bubble-nest Builder
Dwarf Gourami	*Colisa lalia*	India	Bubble-nest Builder
Paradise	*Macropodus opercularis*	China, Burma	Bubble-nest Builder
Rosy Barb	*Puntius conchonius*	India	Egg Layer
Black Ruby	*Puntius nigrofasciatus*	Ceylon	Egg Layer
Sumatranus	*Capoeta tetrazona*	Sumatra	Egg Layer
Zebra	*Brachydanio rerio*	Ceylon	Egg Layer
Pearl Danio	*Brachydanio albolineatus*	Burma	Egg Layer

AQUARIUM
TEMP.   DISPOSITION   FACTS ON BREEDING

70–85	peaceful	Unlike most of the known *Tilapia,* not a mouth-breeder. Eggs laid on solid surface or roots and stems of aquatic plants. Guarded by both parents, who also care for young after hatching.
70–90	wild	Female drops eggs in sand, then picks them all up in her mouth where they are incubated—can't eat during this period. Fry hatch in 2 weeks; rush into mother's mouth whenever disturbed. After a month or so, fish are too large to get into mother's mouth. Males should be removed as soon as female picks up her eggs. Mature in about 1 year.
65–85	peaceful	Spawning pot or stones. Fry hatch 3–5 days and are protected by parent for 2 weeks after which parents should be removed. Mature 6–8 months.
70–90	semiwild	All Gourami breed alike. Male builds bubble nest, female may help. Female is enticed under nest where she drops her eggs. Eggs are picked up by
70–90 70–90	semiwild very peaceful	male and blown into nest. After this phase, remove female. Eggs hatch 2–4 days; male protects young; leave him in tank for 1 week.
60–90	wild	Male is vicious and usually kills a few females before he finds one he likes. Then he builds bubble nest and squeezes eggs from female. He cares for young. Remove female after she drops eggs.
70–80	peaceful and timid	Scatters eggs on plants. Fry hatch 6–8 days. Mature in 9 months.
75–80	peaceful	Same as *P. conchonius.*
70–80	active	Scatter eggs for a few hours, then proceed to eat the spawn. Use dense vegetation. Young mature in 8 months.
45–85	peaceful	Drop nonadhesive eggs. Fry hatch 2–10 days. Feed Infusoria; mature 4–6 months.
50–85	peaceful	Same as Zebra. Mature 7–9 months.

POPULAR NAME	SCIENTIFIC NAME	SOURCE	REPRODUCTION TYPE
Giant Danio	*Danio malabaricus*	Malabar Coast	Egg Layer
"Golly" Barb	*Capoeta oligolepis*	Sumatra	Egg Layer
Blood Fin	*Aphyocharax rubripinnis*	Argentine	Egg Layer
Silver Tetra	*Ctenobrycon spilurus*	Br. Guiana	Egg Layer
Rio Tetra	*Hyphessobrycon flammeus*	Brazil	Egg Layer
Buenos Aires Tetra	*Hemigrammus caudovittatus*	Argentine	Egg Layer
Pristella	*Pristella riddlei*	Venezuela, Br. Guiana	Egg Layer
Butterfly Fish	*Pantodon buchholzi*	West Africa	Egg Layer
Glow Light Tetra	*Hyphessobrycon gracilis*	Guiana	Egg Layer
Neon Tetra	*Paracheirodon innesi*	Amazon River, So. America	Egg Layer
Black-line Tetra	*Hyphessobrycon scholzei*	Lower Amazon	Egg Layer
Blind Cave Fish, or Blind Characin	*Anoptichthys jordani*	Mexico	Egg Layer

AQUARIUM
TEMP.   DISPOSITION   FACTS ON BREEDING

60–85	will eat little fish, otherwise peaceful	Drop very small eggs, some are adhesive. Remove parents after spawning. Need much oxygen.
70–80	peaceful	Lay eggs on plants (Cabomba). Remove parents after spawning. Fry hatch 2–4 days; mature 9–12 months.
70–80	peaceful	Have tall plants and small ones. Fish lay eggs on surface, and as they drop down, get caught on plants. Fry hatch in a day or so.
65–90	too active for community tank	Lay adhesive eggs on fine plants. Eggs should be separated from parents. Fry appear in 3–4 days. Snails eat eggs. Mature 6–8 months.
75–85	very peaceful	Need large tank with plenty of Cabomba. Drop semiadhesive eggs. Remove parents after spawning. Fry hatch in 3 days; mature 8 months.
75–85	more active than Rio Tetra	Same as Rio Tetra. Mature in 10 months.
75–85	peaceful	Spawn on fine plants, adhesive eggs. Remove parents after spawning. Mature in 1 year.
70–80	will eat small fish	A "flying fish." Difficult to breed. Lays large, floating eggs. Fry hatch in 1 week. Fry look like tiny tadpoles, must be fed floating food (mosquito larvae, sifted Daphnia).
70–80	peaceful	Same as Rio Tetra.
70–80	peaceful	Breeding discussed in Chap. IV.
70–80	peaceful	Very adhesive eggs laid on feathery plants; hatch in 24 hours.
low temp.	peaceful	Eggs drop to bottom. Female continues to spawn without male. Remove parents after spawning.

POPULAR NAME	SCIENTIFIC NAME	SOURCE	REPRODUCTION TYPE
Black-winged Hatchet Fish	*Carnegiella marthae*	Amazon & Orinoco rivers, So. America	Egg Layer
Piranha	*Serrasalmus nattereri*	So. America	Egg Layer
Flying Barb	*Esomus danricus*	N. India, Burma	Egg Layer
Black Shark	*Morulius*	Malay Peninsula	Not yet bred
Bitterling	*Rhodeus amarus*	Cen. Europe	Egg Layer
Armored Catfish	*Callichthys callichthys*	N. So. America	Bubble-nest Builder
Whiptail Loricaria	*Loricaria parva*	Paraguay	Egg Layer
Otocinclus	*Otocinclus affinis*	Brazil	Egg Layer
Fundulus chrysotus	*Fundulus chysotus*	So. E. U.S.	Egg Layer
Bluefin	*Chriopeops goodei*	So. E. U.S.	Egg Layer
Cuban Fish	*Cubanichthys cubensis*	Cuba	Egg Layer
Rivulus cylindraceus	*Rivulus cylindraceus*	Cuba	Egg Layer
Red and Blue Rivulus	*Rivulus urophthalmus*	Amazon	Egg Layer

AQUARIUM TEMP.	DISPOSITION	FACTS ON BREEDING
65–85	peaceful	Never been bred.
65–85	very wild	Never been bred.
70–84	active	Must have thickly planted aquarium. Eggs semi-adhesive; hatch in 2 days. Remove parents after spawning.
70–80	peaceful	Not yet bred.
to 70	peaceful	Female inserts ovipositor into gills of a living freshwater mussel and deposits eggs there. Male fish charges surrounding water with sperm which mussel filters through its gills and so fertilizes the eggs. Fry emerge after absorbing their yolk sacs.
70–75	peaceful	Eggs are placed in bubble nest in plants at surface. Parents guard eggs and fry.
75–80	very peaceful	Eggs deposited on top of clean rock. Male guards eggs for incubation period of 8 days.
68–82	peaceful	Eggs laid on glass sides of aquarium; hatch in 48 hours.
70–80	snail killer	Breeds on Myriophyllum. Eggs hatch in 12 days. Fry are easily reared.
70–75	peaceful	Large eggs are suspended in a cluster at end of web-like thread. Thread is caught in plants where eggs are hatched.
70–80	peaceful	Same as Bluefin.
70–80	peaceful	Large eggs are dropped from ovipositor by female on surface. Stock tank with thick plants to prevent parents from eating spawn. Remove parents after spawning.
65–85	peaceful	Same as *Rivulus cylindraceus*.

POPULAR NAME	SCIENTIFIC NAME	SOURCE	REPRODUCTION TYPE
Argentine Pearl Fish	Cynolebias bellottii	Argentina	Egg Layer
Nothobranchius rachovii	Nothobranchius rachovii	Portuguese E. Africa	Egg Layer
Aphyosemion bivittatum	Aphyosemion bivittatum	Tropical W. Africa	Egg Layer
Blue Gularis	Aphyosemion coeruleum	Equatorial W. Africa	Egg Layer
Lyretail	Aphyosemion australe	Cape Lopez Africa	Egg Layer
Panchax chaperi	Epiplatys chaperi	W. Africa	Egg Layer
Mosquito Fish	Heterandria formosa	Southern U.S.	Live Bearer
Guppy	Lebistes reticulatus	Venezuela	Live Bearer
Swordtail	Xiphophorus hellerii	Mexico	Live Bearer
Platy	Xiphophorus maculatus	Mexico	Live Bearer
Molly	Mollienesia Sp.	Southern U.S.	Live Bearer
Geisha Girl Fish	Oryzias latipes	China, Japan and Korea	Egg Layer
Siamese Fighting Fish	Betta splendens	Siam	Bubble-nest Builder
Panchax blockii	Aplocheilus blockii	India	Egg Layer

AQUARIUM TEMP.	DISPOSITION	FACTS ON BREEDING
ca. 70	peaceful	Never bred in tanks.
74–82	peaceful	Nonadhesive eggs hatch in about 100 days. Remove parents after spawning.
70–75	delicate	Eggs are laid among thick plants; hatch in 12 days. Remove parents.
68–72	peaceful	Eggs are deposited singly on bottom; take a long time to hatch. Fry are easily raised.
73–80	peaceful	Eggs are laid on plants such as Riccia. Fry hatch 12–16 days.
65–90	peaceful	About 400 eggs laid during breeding season. Fry hatch in 2 weeks and must be sorted out, as big fry eat little ones. Remove parents after spawning.
65–75	peaceful	Produce several young every few days during breeding season. Fry mature in 6 months.
65–80	peaceful	Produce 30–60 fry every 4–6 weeks. Mature in 4 months.
65–80	peaceful	Produce 10–100 fry every 8 weeks. Mature in 9 months.
65–80	peaceful	Produce 10–100 fry every 4–8 weeks. Mature 6–8 months.
55–80	peaceful	Produce 10–100 fry at irregular intervals. Heavy females are delicate and must be handled carefully.
50–80	peaceful	Eggs hang from female at anal region. Fish seldom bother eggs. Eggs are brushed onto plants. Fry hatch in 2 weeks.
70–90	wild	Male builds large bubble nest. Female forced under nest, and eggs are squeezed from her. Male catches eggs and places them in nest. Fry hatch in 2 days. Male is left in with young for 10 days. Mature in 9 months.
70–80	peaceful	Drop eggs on plants such as Riccia. Mature 7–9 months.

POPULAR NAME	SCIENTIFIC NAME	SOURCE	REPRODUCTION TYPE
Striped Panchax	*Aplocheilus lineatus*	India	Egg Layer
Flag Fish	*Jordanella floridae*	Florida	Egg Layer
Blue Poecilia	*Limia caudofasciata*	Jamaica	Live Bearer
Mollienesia velifera	*Mollienesia velifera*	Yucatan	Live Bearer
Sailfin or Molly	*Mollienesia latipinna*	Gulf Coast, N.E. Mexico	Live Bearer
Black or Midnight Mollies	Black Mollienesias	All Black Mollienesias were originally line bred from rare natural black freaks, occurring mostly among the *latipinna* species. Young when born are sometimes light, and sometimes dark. When an inch long, they begin turning black; some turn black in 6 months, some take longer, some never do. "Permablacks" are a type developed through persistent selective breeding; this type is born black and remains so.	
Half-beak	*Dermogenys pusillus*	Malay Peninsula	Live Bearer
Three-spined Stickleback	*Gasterosteus aculeatus*	Coastal waters or N. Atlantic & N. Pacific	Egg Layer
Australian Rainbow Fish	*Nematocentrus nigrans*	Australia	Egg Layer
Badis badis	*Badis badis*	India	Egg Layer

AQUARIUM TEMP.	DISPOSITION	FACTS ON BREEDING
70–80	peaceful	Same as *Epiplatys chaperi.*
70–75	rather wild	Stock tank thickly, especially with Riccia and soft algae. Eggs are dropped to bottom and hatch in 5–6 days. Male guards and fans eggs.
68–75	peaceful	Parents eat fry. Young should be protected, as it is a species worth cultivating.
68–75	peaceful	Broods run as high as 100. Remove parents after spawning.
70–80	peaceful	Isolate heavy females in well-planted 10- or more gallon tank. Handle as little and as gently as possible; dead or defective fry are result of handling. All Mollies should be handled as little as possible.
70–75	peaceful	Breed in shallow water; a teaspoonful of salt added to the gallon is helpful, as many of the fry are born dead.
65–70	wild	Lays eggs in hole dug in sand; male guards eggs, which hatch in 4 days.
60–90	very peaceful	Breed very rapidly, should be fed continuously with live food. Fry can be left with parents.
75–85	peaceful	Spawn upside down on inside of flowerpot. Eggs hatch in 2 days. Will eat only live food.

POPULAR NAME	SCIENTIFIC NAME	SOURCE	REPRODUCTION TYPE
Polycentropsis abbreviata	*Polycentropsis abbreviata*	Gulf of Guinea	Egg Layer
Polycentrus schomburgkii	*Polycentrus schomburgkii*	W. Indies	Egg Layer
Chocolate Cichlid	*Cichlasoma coryphaenoides*	Brazil	Egg Layer
Leaf Fish	*Monocirrhus polyacanthus*	Amazon, Guiana	Egg Layer
Giant or Striped Gourami	*Colisa fasciata*	India	Egg Layer
Thick-lipped Gourami	*Colisa labiosa*	Burma	Bubble-nest Builder
Pearl Gourami	*Trichogaster leeri*	Siam, Malay Peninsula, Sumatra	Bubble-nest Builder

AQUARIUM TEMP.	DISPOSITION	FACTS ON BREEDING
70–80	will eat small fish	Male blows bubbles on tops of leaves, such as Cabomba; female deposits about 100 eggs on plant among bubbles. Remove female after spawning.
70–85	peaceful	Tank must be partially shaded during breeding with a screen of plants. Spawn inside a flowerpot laid on its side, with opening toward a darkened corner, away from aquarist's view. Remove female after spawning. Male fans eggs, which hatch in 4 days. Remove him after eggs hatch.
70–85	wild	From the social standpoint, Cichlids have the most highly developed breeding habits. Prior to breeding, the parents dig holes in the sand of the breeding tank. A flat, preferably light-colored stone is selected for deposition of eggs and it is cleaned and polished with utmost care by both parents. When all this is ready, the female goes to the stone and deposits a few eggs on it with her ovipositor. The male then fertilizes them. This is repeated until 100 to 2,000 eggs are laid. Eggs are slightly adhesive. Spawning completed, both parents take turns fanning the eggs. When fungus attacks eggs, those affected eggs are eaten by parents to avoid spreading of infection. Eggs hatch in 4 days. Just before or after hatching, parents carry eggs in their mouths to holes dug in the sand, moving them from one hole to another. After 4–10 days, fry emerge after absorbing yolk sacs. As a rule, Cichlids are wild and should be in a tank by themselves or in a community tank with large fish. Efforts at breeding the Chocolate Cichlids end mostly in killings.
75–80	peaceful	Breeding somewhat similar to that of Cichlids. Remove parents after spawning.
75–80	peaceful	Rudimentary bubble nest blown by male. Eggs are lighter than water and float. Fry hatch in 2 days. Remove female after spawning, and male 3 days after eggs hatch.
75–80	peaceful	Same as *Colisa fasciata*.
65–85	peaceful	Same as *Colisa fasciata*.

POPULAR NAME	SCIENTIFIC NAME	SOURCE	REPRODUCTION TYPE
Snakeskin Gourami	*Trichogaster pectoralis*	Siam, Malay Peninsula, Fr. Indo-China	Bubble-nest Builder
Kissing Gourami	*Helostoma temmincki*	Malay Peninsula	Egg Layer
Large Mouth-breeder	*Tilapia macrocephala*	Gold Coast to So. Nigeria	Egg Layer
Texas Cichlid	*Herichthys cyanoguttatus*	Mexico, Texas	Egg Layer
Firemouth	*Cichlasoma meeki*	Yucatan	Egg Layer
Cuban Cichlid	*Cichlasoma tetracanthus*	Cuba	Egg Layer
Cichlasoma severum	*Cichlasoma severum*	Amazon	Egg Layer
Acara or Festivum	*Cichlasoma festivum*	Amazon	Egg Layer
Jack Dempsey	*Cichlasoma biocellatum*	So. America	Egg Layer
Kongo Cichlid	*Cichlasoma nigrofasciatum*	So. America	Egg Layer
Blue Acara	*Aequidens latifrons*	Panama Colombia	Egg Layer
Aequidens curviceps	*Aequidens curviceps*	Amazon	Egg Layer
Keyhole Fish	*Aequidens maronii*	Br. Guiana, Venezuela	Egg Layer
Aequidens portalegrensis	*Aequidens portalegrensis*	S.E. Brazil	Egg Layer
Astronotus ocellatus	*Astronotus ocellatus*	Cen. America	Egg Layer

AQUARIUM TEMP.	DISPOSITION	FACTS ON BREEDING
68–85	peaceful	Typical bubble-nest builder. Spawns are very large. Parents will not disturb fry.
75–82	peaceful	Lays 400–2000 eggs which float to surface. Young hatch in 1 day.
68–85	peaceful	Same as Egyptian Mouthbreeder, except that male carries young.
65–82	peaceful	Breeding typical of Cichlids.
70–80	wild	Breeding typical of Cichlids.
75–80	rough on plants	Breeding similar to type, but female does most of the courting.
75–80	peaceful	Standard breeding of Cichlids.
75–82	peaceful	Same as *Cichlasoma severum*.
65–90	wild	Standard breeding of Cichlids.
70–80	wild	Breed like other Cichlids. Female cares for eggs.
70–85	peaceful	Breeds true to Cichlid habits.
74–78	timid	Hard to breed. Privacy required for breeding. They do not tear up plants. Remove parents after spawning.
70–80	peaceful	Breeds true to Cichlid habits.
70–80	peaceful	Easy to breed; breeds true to Cichlid habits.
70–80	wild	Hard to breed; breeds like other Cichlids. Remove parents after spawning.

POPULAR NAME	SCIENTIFIC NAME	SOURCE	REPRODUCTION TYPE
Pompadour Fish, Disc Cichlid	*Symphysodon discus*	Amazon	Egg Layer
Ramirezi	*Apistogramma ramirezi*	Venezuela	Egg Layer
Apistogramma agassizi	*Apistogramma agassizi*	Unknown	Egg Layer
Dascyllus trimaculatus	*Dascyllus trimaculatus*	Red Sea to E. Indies, Hawaii	Egg Layer
Black-and-white Damsel Fish	*Dascyllus aruanus*	E. Indies to S. Pacific Islands	Egg Layer
Blue Devil	*Pomacentrus fuscus*	Florida, W. Indies	Egg Layer
Clownfish	*Amphiprion percula*	Coral reefs of Indo-Pacific	Egg Layer
Neotoca bilineata	*Neotoca bilineata*	Mexico	Live Bearer
Gambusia	*Gambusia affinis*	Southern Coast States	Live Bearer
Blue Gambusia	*Gambusia punctata*	Cuba	Live Bearer
Belonesox	*Belonesox belizanus*	Cen. America	Live Bearer
Pseudoxipho-phorus	*Pseudoxipho-phorus bimac-ulatus*	Cen. America	Live Bearer

AQUARIUM TEMP.	DISPOSITION	FACTS ON BREEDING
70–85	too large for community tank	Breed like Angel Fish, *Pterophyllum scalare*. Remove eggs from parents and aerate them. Eggs hatch in 3 days at temperature of 84° F. They should be kept at this temperature in shallow, slightly acid water for a month, and be given mild aeration. Parents will eat eggs.
70–80	rather timid	A dwarf Cichlid; breeds like larger Cichlids; unlike other dwarf Cichlids in which female alone guards eggs.
70–80	rather timid	Remove male after spawning.
70–75	rather wild	A marine fish, preferring ocean water. Breeding habits unknown.
70–75	semiwild	A marine fish. Will live in community tank in fresh water. Breeding habits unknown.
70–80	active	Will deposit eggs on inside of large empty shells, and care for young in same manner as Cichlids.
70–75	active	Adhesive eggs laid on solid surface and cared for in manner of Cichlids. Young not cared for, however.
70–77	peaceful	Has 5 broods per year under good conditions; 5–40 fry, according to size of female. Fry mature 3–6 months.
40–100	wild	Very prolific; fry develop very fast.
68–75	peaceful	Not prolific; will eat fry. Remove parents after spawning.
72–85	very wild	Clear old water desirable for breeding. Young are ¾ inch long when born and are ready for eating full-sized Daphnia at once.
68–82	wild	Remove parents after spawning and separate male and female, as female will attack male. Young develop very rapidly.

POPULAR NAME	SCIENTIFIC NAME	SOURCE	REPRODUCTION TYPE
Phalloceros	*Phalloceros caudomaculatus*	Brazil	Live Bearer
Merry Widow	*Phallichthys amates*	Honduras	Live Bearer
Phallichthys pittieri	*Phallichthys isthmensis*	Panama	Live Bearer
Poecilistes pleurospilus	*Poecilistes pleurospilus*	Cen. America	Live Bearer
Girardinus metallicus	*Girardinus metallicus*	Cuba	Live Bearer
Quintana atrizona	*Quintana atrizona*	Cuba, Isle of Pines	Live Bearer
Poecilia vivipara	*Poecilia vivipara*	N. So. Amer., Puerto Rico, So. Brazil	Live Bearer
Limia melanogaster	*Limia melanogaster*	Jamaica	Live Bearer
Glassfish	*Chanda lala*	India	Egg Layer
Archer Fish	*Toxotes jaculatrix*	E. Indies	Unknown
Spotted Scat	*Scatophagus argus*	E. Indies	Unknown
Fresh-water Sole	*Trinectes maculatus*	Coastal water from Cape Cod southward	Unknown
Blow Fish	*Tetraodon fluviatilis*	India, Burma, Malay Peninsula	Egg Layer

AQUARIUM TEMP.	DISPOSITION	FACTS ON BREEDING
55–75	peaceful	Easy to breed and very prolific.
68–75	lively	Free breeders.
70–80	peaceful	Moderately fertile; easy to breed and feed.
70–84	peaceful	Fairly good breeder.
68–84	peaceful	An active fish, though not likely to eat fry.
73–80	peaceful	About 20 fry at each breeding. If kept at temperature of 75° F. or higher and given live and prepared foods alternately, it is possible to mature them to breeding size in 16 weeks.
68–82	peaceful	Easy to breed and feed.
70–75	active	Not a hardy fish.
75–80	peaceful	Hard to breed. Use old water, about 4 inches deep, with surface well spread with Riccia. Eggs are discharged upward into plants from an upside-down position. Remove parents after spawning.
70–80	peaceful	Breeding habits unknown.
70–78	peaceful	Breeding habits unknown.
60–72	semiwild	Not bred.
70–80	very active	Adhesive eggs placed on rocks, etc., to be guarded and cared for.

Bibliography

Selected Bibliography on Tropical Fresh-water Fish and Their Maintenance

Arnold, Joh. Paul, and Ernst Ahl, *Fremdländische Süsswasserfische*, Gustav Wenzel, Braunschweig, 1936.

*Axelrod, Herbert R., and others, *Exotic Tropical Fishes*, T.F.H. Publications, Jersey City, 1962.

*Axelrod, Herbert R., and Shaw, Susan, *Breeding Aquarium Fishes*, T.F.H. Publications, Jersey City, 1967.

*Axelrod, Herbert R., and Vorderwinkler, William, *Encyclopedia of Tropical Fish*, T.F.H. Publications, Jersey City, 1966.

*Besnard, Wladimir, *Capture et Acclimatation des Poissons Exotiques*, Payot, Paris, 1938.

*Coates, Christopher W., *Tropical Fishes as Pets*, rev. ed., Liveright Publishing Corp., New York, 1950.

*Curtis, Brian, *The Life Story of the Fish*, Harcourt, Brace and Company. Inc., New York, 1949.

*Fraser-Brunner, Alex, *The Guppy: An Aquarist Booklet*, Buckley Press, Brentford, Middlesex, 1946.

*Frey, Hans, *Illustrated Dictionary of Tropical Fishes*, T.F.H. Publications, Jersey City, 1961.

*Innes, William T., *Exotic Aquarium Fishes*, T.F.H. Publications, Jersey City, 1968.

*Norman, J. R., *A History of Fishes*, reprint, A. A. Wyn, Inc., New York, 1948.

Roule, Louis, *Fishes, Their Journeys and Migrations*, W. W. Norton & Company, New York, 1933.

*Schultz, Leonard P., and Edith M. Stern, *The Ways of Fishes*, D. Van Nostrand Company, Inc., New York, 1948.

Stoye, Frederick H., *Tropical Fishes for the Home*, 2d ed., Carl Mertens, New York, 1935.

* At present in print.

Selected Bibliography on Tropical Marine Fish and Their Maintenance

Axelrod, Herbert R., and Vorderwinkler, William, *Salt Water Aquarium Fish*, T.F.H. Publications, Jersey City, 1963.

Beebe, William, and John Tee-Van, *Field Book of the Shore Fishes of Bermuda*, G. P. Putnam's Sons, New York, 1933.

*Breder, C. M., Jr., *Field Book of Marine Fishes of the Atlantic Coast*, rev. ed., G. P. Putnam's Sons, New York, 1948.

*Coker, R. E., *This Great and Wide Sea*, 1947.

Crowder, William, *Between the Tides*, Dodd, Mead & Company, Inc., New York, 1931.

Flattely, Fred W., and Charles L. Walton, *Biology of the Seashore*, The Macmillan Company, New York, 1922.

Gardener, Bernard J., *Marine Aquaria: Their Care and Maintenance*, privately printed, New York, 1949.

*Innes, William T., *Exotic Aquarium Fishes*, 11th ed., Innes Publishing Company, Philadelphia, 1950.

Johnson, Myrtle E., and Harry J. Snook, *Seashore Animals of the Pacific Coast*, The Macmillan Company, New York, 1927.

*MacGinitie, G. E., and Nettie MacGinitie, *Natural History of Marine Animals*, McGraw-Hill Publishing Company, Inc., New York, 1949.

*Palmer, E. Laurence, *Fieldbook of Natural History*, McGraw-Hill Book Company, Inc., 1949.

Randall, John E., *Caribbean Reef Fishes*, T.F.H. Publications, Jersey City, 1968.

*Ricketts, Edward F., and Jack Calvin, *Between Pacific Tides*, rev. ed., Stanford, Palo Alto, 1948.

Roughley, T. C., *Wonders of the Great Barrier Reef*, Charles Scribner's Sons, New York, 1947.

*Russell, F. S., and C. M. Yonge, *The Seas*, Frederick Warne & Co., Inc., New York, 1947.

*Sverdrup, H. U., Martin W. Johnson, and Richard H. Fleming, *The Oceans*, Prentice-Hall, Inc., New York, 1942.

*Yonge, C. M., *The Sea Shore*, William Collins Sons & Company, Canada, Ltd., Toronto, 1949.

Periodicals in English on Tropical Fish and Their Maintenance

The Aquarium (Monthly) Pet Books Incorporated, 87 Rt. 17, Maywood, N.J., 07607 ($2.50 per year, 35 cents per copy).

The Aquarist and Pondkeeper (Monthly) The Butts, Half Acre, Brentford, Middlesex, United Kingdom ($2.50 per year).

Tropical Fish Hobbyist (Monthly) T.F.H. Publications, Inc. 245 Cornelison Ave., Jersey City, N.J. 07302 ($4.00 per year, 40 cents per copy).

* At present in print.

General Index

[Scientific names of fish are listed
in index beginning on page 297.]

Index of
Scientific Names

[Popular names of fish are listed
in index beginning on page 287.]